HORIZON

SEPTEMBER, 1958 • VOLUME I, NUMBER 1

FOREWORD

Much have I travell'd in the realms of gold,
And many goodly states and kingdoms seen . . .

Thus, "On first looking into Chapman's Homer" was Keats transfigured by the beauty to which man may aspire, by the splendor of his achievements, by the poignancy of his failures, and by thoughts "too deep for tears." It is in this sonnet that he brings us across the horizon of history and down the long chasm of the centuries to our own beginnings, to

stout Cortez, when with eagle eyes
He stared at the Pacific—and all his men
Look'd at each other with a wild surmise—
Silent, upon a peak in Darien.

We take for our title the word *horizon* because it is here, where earth and sky meet, that one may observe those jagged interruptions in the landscape that are the works of man: the squat mud houses of ancient Sumer; the gleaming statuary of the isles of Greece; the stately sky line of Venice when "she did hold the gorgeous East in fee"; a perfect bridge in Peking; our own soaring, protean civilization; all that moved Milton to write that

Towred Cities please us then,
And the busie humm of men.

Culture, the concern of this new magazine, is both achievement and dream, a work of the hands and a movement of the spirit, the special property of man since the great miracle of the Sixth Day—since Darwin's hairy quadruped dropped from his tree and (how many millennia later?) first lifted up his gaze to seek something beyond mere food and drink. Culture is art and ideas, past and present, taken in sum as a guide to life. It is history too, the science which Dionysius tells us is "philosophy teaching by examples," with philosophy suspended between the *I-believe* of theology and the *I-know* of science. It is the concern of writers who fill libraries with it, of poets who leave it "apparell'd in celestial light," of dramatists who represent it, of scientists who analyze it, of gifted men who chip and paint and mold their vision of the truth which lies, never fully revealed, within the complex whole. Culture, finally, is a birthright which we all inherit, the heritage man carries with him on his earthly voyage.

The caravel on the opposite page was painted by Pieter Brueghel in 1557, when the Age of Exploration was under full sail. No lovelier ship has ever been portrayed, and we choose it for our frontispiece because it seems to symbolize that remarkable chapter of modern history in which the adventuring genius of Western Europe set forth, freighted with all the treasures of the classical Hellenic world and of Christian civilization, to seek a new Zion across the Western ocean.

The genius of Brueghel, the son of Flemish peasants, took fire in some measure from the great sun of the Italian Renaissance, which had reached its zenith half a century earlier, and his genius in turn helped to kindle, half a century later, the artistic blaze of the young Dutch Republic. The story of that incandescent era in the Netherlands is told in this opening issue of HORIZON by C. V. Wedgwood and illustrated with some of the luminous art it produced. It was a triumph of pure spirit for a people who had little to start with except, as the historian Taine observed, "a salt mudbank on the North Sea." The Dutch were a business people, much like ourselves, and it may be worth noting that their glory in the world of painting went hand in hand with their greatest commercial and military triumphs.

We may also observe the heartening fact, in a time of trouble like our own, that Holland's greatness was achieved in an era of peril and uncertainty. The Attic light never shone so clear as under the threat of Persian might; Rome's greatest orators and poets lived—and were banished and proscribed—amid fierce civil strife. The proud power of Spain threatened Shakespeare's England, and during the Great Age of Exploration, as H. R. Trevor-Roper points out in his article in this issue, most of Western Europe trembled before the dark forces of the East that stood at the gates of Vienna.

History speaks to us often in riddles, with a Delphic voice. Yet it is clear that we in America today are the inheritors of many a great golden age, heirs to much of the glory that was Greece and the grandeur that was Rome, and to the strength of a little island off the coast of Europe which bestowed poetry, literature, manners, and certain explosive ideas of freedom on half the earth. Whether, as some of our critics say, America is a kind of Rome and will never match the artistic and cultural achievements of Greece's modern counterpart—England and Western Europe—no one may assert with assurance. Nor can any man say as yet whether it is time to sing a recessional or chant a magnificat for the United States at what seems from a historical standpoint its moment of greatest magnificence.

This magazine in any case is commenced in the belief that some better guide than now exists in America is needed to the house of culture, with all its thousands of rooms. Never has there been in history such an opportunity to explore this imposing edifice, or so wide a horizon open to our sight. The world is suddenly grown very small, and its treasures are visible to all. Never has so much been known about art and culture in all parts of time and space, never have so many of us, it would seem, had such an appetite for knowledge, or for travel in Keats' realms of gold.

Such is the field we choose. We intend to pay attention to those aspects of life peculiar to high civilizations—to art and ideas; to the study of man and nature; to letters; to manners and customs; and, in the long view, to political and scientific subjects as they affect civilized man. HORIZON will have no limits in time or geography. It will deal with a past known only to the archaeologist or the myth teller. And it will treat of the great non-Western cultures which have existed so long, so far away, and are now in the twentieth century thrown so suddenly into contact with the West.

But the great concern of HORIZON will be with our own civilization, Modern Western variety, No. 21 in Professor Toynbee's grand catalogue of history, the culture pattern born in the dim Mediterranean past, shaped in modern Europe and brought across the unknown and terrifying horizon by brave men in little ships to find—and found—a new citadel in North America.

We invite all those whose interests lie in this broad field, whether as contributors or readers, to join us in this venture.

The Editors

HORIZON
A Magazine of the Arts

SEPTEMBER, 1958 · VOLUME I, NUMBER 1

PUBLISHER
James Parton

EDITOR
Joseph J. Thorndike, Jr.

MANAGING EDITOR
William Harlan Hale

ASSISTANT EDITORS
Margery Darrell
Hilde Heun
Ada Pesin
Jane Wilson

EDITORIAL ASSISTANTS
Robert C. Agee, Caroline Backlund,
Gertrudis Feliu, Mary Ann Pfeiffer
Nancy Teass, Martha Thomson

ART DIRECTOR
Irwin Glusker

Assistant: Richard B. Browner

ADVISORY BOARD
Gilbert Highet, *Chairman*
Frederick Burkhardt   Oliver Jensen
Marshal B. Davidson   Jotham Johnson
Alfred Frankfurter   Richard M. Ketchum
J. H. Plumb

CIRCULATION DIRECTOR
Richard V. Benson

HORIZON is published every two months by
American Horizon, Inc., a subsidiary of American
Heritage Publishing Co., Inc., 551 Fifth Avenue,
New York 17, N. Y.
Single Copies: $3.95
Annual Subscriptions: $18.00 in the U.S.A.
$19.00 elsewhere

Application for Second-Class mail privileges is
pending at New York, N. Y.

HORIZON welcomes contributions but can assume
no responsibility for such unsolicited material.

COVER: Few early balloonists' flights attracted more attention than the one that carried
Mrs. Letitia Ann Sage aloft from London in 1785 as the first Englishwoman to brave the
skies. Our cover painting, *The Three Favorite Aerial Travellers*, done that same year by J. F.
Rigaud, presents the scene—with one major inaccuracy. As shown here, Mrs. Sage's companions were Mr. George Biggin, a fellow passenger also on his first flight, and, resplendent
in the uniform of the Honourable Artillery Company, the Italian aeronaut Lunardi,
already famous as the first man to make an ascent in England. At the last moment before
take-off, though, pilot Lunardi found that the balloon would not lift all three together and
so stayed behind and let his passengers soar away on their own. They landed an hour
later in a field at Harrow. An article on ballooning begins on page 114. The picture is reproduced through the courtesy of Peninsular and Oriental Steam Navigation Company.

By WILFRID NOYCE

WHY MEN SEEK ADVENTURE

A British mountaineer explores the many motives that have led men to try their

strength and wit against peaks, jungles, deserts, arctic ice, and the ocean's floor

Last year, in the twilight of a Himalayan June, I sat below a mountain in Nepal. It had been nearly a year since we first knew that we were coming to try and climb this peak of some 23,000 feet; nearly a year of thought and care and preparation culminating in a six weeks' struggle with the hardest snow and ice problem any of us had ever faced. Why had we done it? And how had this great beetling tower come to loom so large in our lives?

Many of my mountaineering friends have a ready answer to this question. One, after reading an article on "Why I climb," threw down the paper in disgust, exclaiming: "What rubbish! I climb because I like it. Isn't that enough?" Of course it is, for most; and equally of course the great majority of climbers, divers, cavers, and other suchlike cranks would give no more than that answer if asked why they pursued their favorite madness. But the answer never really satisfied me; at least it left me with an uneasy sense that it was too easy.

I have been climbing mountains since I was eight and

"BECAUSE IT'S THERE" That was George Mallory's classic answer to the question why he wanted to climb a mountain. Actually many motives draw men to places like the Himalayan landscape on the facing page. Reaching the end of his climb to a lower summit, the mountaineer comes within sight of the towering peak of Nanda Devi.

seldom really stopped to consider what I was doing or why I did it. But I thought now that maybe I would solve some of my incipient queries by looking at those that face the balloonist, the flier, the Arctic explorer. It seemed at first ridiculous that one could analyze motives and push them into compartments, as one might pour chemicals into test tubes. But as I studied my own adventure, mountaineering, and read more about others, the figures began curiously to fit themselves into certain patterns. Obviously, the same person may be affected by a number of different motives, in the same way that a single motive may impel very different people. And yet, at the end of it all, a few very broad lines did seem to stick out, like the primary colors in a painting that explain all the confusing blends. And once I had accepted my artificial convention, as one accepts a convention of the theater, it was surprising how many adventurers did, with a squeeze, fit their compartments—provided that I chuckled as I did the squeezing and reminded myself that it was all a game anyway.

It will perhaps be simplest to take one or two people who seem to represent well each type of motive. This will place everything in far too sharp a black and white. No matter, so long as we remain conscious of the infinity of grays all round. These people, it will be found, all come from the nineteenth or twentieth centuries, and for a reason.

7

It seemed, as I read, that only since about 1800 had adventure for its own sake crystallized in men's minds. In early explorers (with exceptions like Marco Polo, though even he was a merchant, and that other Italian, Lodovico di Varthema) motives were, broadly speaking, interwoven with ideas of trade, Northwest passages, empire, colonization, and the like. And there was always war in the background as an alternative adventure. But by 1815 war had lost almost all attraction it might have had; and the alternative, for the individual, became travel and kindred adventure. It may be that men, looking back, will regard the nineteenth and twentieth centuries to our day as the golden age of adventure on this planet. For in those years, partly for gain perhaps but also "for their own sakes," the great rivers were followed up, the continents mapped. The seas were sailed in smaller as well as larger boats, and the mysteries of the undersea world revealed. The highest mountains were climbed, the deepest caves plumbed. The Poles were reached, the Antarctic explored (very partially as yet). Flight, the dream of Leonardo da Vinci, was realized and pursued even to the stratosphere and above. Much of this was done quite simply "because it's there," in George Mallory's phrase. Perhaps the golden age is drawing to a close, for the private adventurer at least. Science is consolidating the gains of spectacular amateurs, and with science there return once more politics and the desires of empire. But I am straying from the motives of the individuals.

The Lure of Hardship

The first adventurer I have in mind is the man who does a thing, partly at any rate, because he does not enjoy it: the man who, in the Middle Ages, would have worn a hair shirt next to his skin. Here is the Winter Journey, undertaken in 1911 by Wilson, Bowers, and Cherry-Garrard through the Antarctic night to obtain embryos of the emperor penguin from Cape Crozier:

The horror of the nineteen days it took us to travel from Cape Evans to Cape Crozier would have to be re-experienced to be appreciated; and anyone would be a fool who went again.... It was the darkness that did it. I don't believe minus seventy temperatures would be bad in daylight, not comparatively bad, when you could see where you were going, where you were stepping, where the sledge straps were, the cooker, the primus, the food; could read a

JEAN-JACQUES LANGUEPIN

THE AUTHOR   Wilfrid Noyce, photographed above on Mount Everest, was a member of the British team that climbed Everest in 1953. A poet and novelist as well as a writer of nonfiction, he is now at work on a book exploring the motivations of the adventurer. Entitled THE SPRINGS OF ADVENTURE, *it will be published by The World Publishing Company next spring.*

compass without striking three or four boxes to find one dry match; could read your watch to see if the blissful moment of getting out of your bag was come without groping in the snow all about; when it would not take you five minutes to lash up the door of the tent and five hours to get started.

But in these days we were never less than four hours from the moment when Bill cried "Time to get up" to the time when we got into our harness. It took two men to get one man into his harness, and was all they could do, for the canvas was frozen and our clothes were frozen until sometimes not even two men could bend them into the required shape.*

The temperature dropped to 77.5 degrees below zero. After terrible escapes and obstacles, they had got three eggs and managed to build an igloo. Then, their tent was blown bodily away (it was recovered later by a miracle) and the igloo roof was torn off although it was held down by large snow blocks. They lay in the open, drifted over with snow, without a meal for over thirty-six hours. "The journey had beggared our language: no words could express its horror."

There is in all these forms of physical enterprise a certainty, accepted consciously, that you will have to suffer and a possibility, to be discussed later, that you may have to die. Apart from this there is usually an acceptance of sheer physical strain. Joshua Slocum, the first man to sail alone round the world, fought four days of continuous storm as he came out of the Straits of Magellan. Alain Gerbault, the first man to sail directly east to west across the Atlantic alone, spent seventeen and eighteen hours at the tiller, sometimes steering with his feet so that he could repair sails. African explorers like Mungo Park walked until they dropped from thirst. Sven Hedin endured four days without water in the Takla Makan desert of Asia. Sir Ernest Shackleton faced sixteen days almost without sleep in his small boat, with clothes drenched by day and frozen at night, on the last stage of his Antarctic journey. Hermann Buhl made, with the help only of drugs, his astonishing lone ascent of about 4,000 feet to the summit of Nanga Parbat in the Himalayas. Men know, when they go out, that they may have to face these things.

Why do they do it? Of course you can maintain that much of this hardship was endured in the cause of science. People measure ice caps, collect emperor penguins' eggs, and even sit under the snow for months, in order to add to the sum of the world's meteorological knowledge. But that seems to me only very partially the answer. I think that

* The Worst Journey in the World, by Apsley Cherry-Garrard (Constable, 1922).

the reasons are many, and that one of them is simply that it is part of the human make-up to want to "prove" yourself, to show yourself that you can do something you thought impossible. But if you take it one further, you may conclude that this kind of controlled toughness stems out of the pleasure one gets from proving and hence mastering all one's faculties. Moreover, by mastering and toughening himself so that he can extend his limits far beyond what he believed possible, a man has at the back of his mind also the feeling that he is on the way to mastering the world. There will be "nothing that he cannot do." My favorite example of this feeling is Robert Falcon Scott of the Antarctic.

Scott is much misunderstood. He is either idolized for heroism or condemned for inefficiency. He was not, it seems to me, either a hero (a meaningless term) nor inefficient. He was a man who started with all the disadvantages and made of himself a great leader. If the luck of the weather had gone for him as it went for Sir Vivian Fuchs last March, he would have been hailed as a triumphant organizer into the bargain. Frail as a boy, and nervous and irritable too, Scott used his opportunities, elsewhere and in the Antarctic, to discipline body and mind. It was a grim discipline, as we can see from the Southern Journey undertaken during the *Discovery* expedition (1901–4). With Wilson and Shackle-

ton he set out on a man-hauling trip into the interior. "One perceives that this was nothing but a voluntary exile of three months' hard labour, in which extreme discomfort was the only relief to excessive toil, and toil the only mitigation of discomfort," George Seaver wrote.* Shackleton almost died of scurvy and the other two, both previous invalids, finished by dragging him back on the sleigh. On the Polar Journey of 1910–12 Scott drove himself as hard as the others. He would often push on an hour beyond stopping time; as one member of the party remarked, "even a blizzard had its silver lining." In the end, he outlasted four very strong men.

The wearing of a physical hair shirt was symbolic of a deeper mastery, that of himself. In *The Worst Journey in the World*, Apsley Cherry-Garrard wrote: "Scott was the strongest combination of a strong man in a strong body that I have ever known. And this because he was so weak! Naturally so peevish, highly strung, irritable, depressed and moody. Practically such a conquest of himself, such vitality, such push and determination, and withal in himself such personal and magnetic charm . . . he conquered his weaker self and became the stronger leader whom we went to follow and came to love."

"By endurance I conquer" was the Shackletons' family

* *Edward Wilson of the Antarctic*, by George Seaver (Murray, 1933).

PAUL POPPER, LTD.

"IT IS RIGHT FOR SOME OF US TO GO TO THE ENDS OF THE EARTH"
The last team to reach the South Pole by the overland route until Sir Edmund Hillary's success in 1958
was the Scott party of 1912 (left to right: Oates, Bowers, Scott, Wilson, Evans). They died returning.

"A SHEER LOVE OF THE LIFE"
To Lindbergh in 1927, an unspanned At-
lantic Ocean was irresistible. The promise
of great fame was pleasant but secondary.

motto. What do I conquer? I conquer myself, and by so doing I set out to conquer the world. I achieve, against all obstacles, something that may be practically useful or may not. And by achieving it I add something indefinable but precious to the sum of life.

The Lure of Contrast

The austerity of wearing the hair shirt is tempered by the contrasting pleasure of taking it off. To undergo discomfort simply for the pleasure of being comfortable again would be too like the man who beat his head against a stone because it would be so nice when he stopped. But the pleasure of contrast undoubtedly comes high in the list of component pleasures savored artfully by the traveler. "No one," Livingstone exclaimed, "can truly appreciate the charm of repose unless he has undergone extreme exertion."

Gino Watkins, who was leading his fourth Arctic expedition at the time he lost his life in a kayak at twenty-five, looked to most an easy-going undergraduate. And he was a successful leader partly just because he had this playboy air about him. His companions all thought they could do better than such an unserious young man, found they could not, and tried the harder. Yet his enjoyment of unserious London was as genuine as that of serious Greenland. Before starting on the Arctic Air-Route Expedition of 1930–31, he missed none of the dances of the London season. Often he visited two or three in a single night, ran home—this running was his exercise—and appeared spruce and ready for work a few hours later.

I believe that the liking for contrast stems from a deeper need than the purely physical. Luxury and hardship—these are both facets of life, and it is difficult to appreciate the one without having experienced the other. Not everybody

can live both lives successfully as Watkins did, winning the most from both. Some become permanently restless and dissatisfied with the return. But to those who can readjust, "a new vision of the world won through hardship" is waiting.

The Lure of Danger

Another self-proving motive is the desire for danger. I used to think that nobody, apart from the enthusiasts who roll themselves over the Niagara in barrels, could really find danger a bait. But it seems to me now, firstly, that to a few danger is quite distinctly an inducement; secondly, that to a great majority it is accepted as an inevitable part of a worthwhile adventure, then minimized by skill; and thirdly, that to almost everyone the whiff of danger, more apparent than real, which we call "thrill," is a spice to season the mildest donkey ride or canoe outing. When Richard Hillary flew under the Severn Bridge during the last war, he felt he must do it because somebody else had done it. But his friend Peter Pease said:

"Richard, from now on a lot of people are going to fly under that bridge. From a flying point of view it proves nothing: it's extremely stupid. From a personal point of view it can only be of value if you don't tell anybody about it."

Hillary adds:

He was right, of course. To fly under the bridge now simply to come back and say that I had done so would be sheer exhibitionism. It would prove nothing. Yet I knew I would fly under it. I had to for my own satisfaction, just as many years before I had had to stand on a twenty-five-foot board above a swimming pool until I had dived off. *

He did it, with inches to spare, and said nothing. The initial impulse was of bravado, or sheer courage. Then he did it from a motive akin to that discussed earlier, to prove to himself that he *could* do it (the reason suggested by Peter Pease). He did it also, I think, like the other fliers, because it was part of the total experience of flying. He would have missed something without it; just as the rock climber may feel that he must do everything in the scale, even a dangerous solo ascent, not because he wants to but because he might, if he did not, miss something in the gamut of emotions—perhaps something that would have suited him exactly.

Somewhere near this experience come some of the earlier flying feats, like Lindbergh's air-circus parachute jumps. In the early twenties flying itself was thought dangerous, wing walking and parachute jumping suicidal. Yet he did both, barnstorming up and down the country, billed as "Daredevil Lindbergh," getting people to pay money to see him jump. Why? He answers, enigmatically and yet understandably too: "I believe the risks I take are justified by the sheer love of the life I lead." And he argues that even in those early days

* *The Last Enemy*, by Richard Hillary (St. Martins, 1943).

the risks were far less than they seemed (that is a quality of danger) and that this is even more the case on the Atlantic flight. "Of course there's danger; but a certain amount of danger is essential to the quality of life. I don't believe in taking foolish chances; but nothing can be accomplished without taking any chance at all."*

That is to say Lindbergh, like the mountain guide who writes, "We loved our life as we loved our jobs," considered dispassionately that his job—in this case the flight from New York to Paris of 1927—was worth the risk, which he could largely control by skillful flying and which itself was part of the total worthwhile experience. "Yes, just being in the air on a flight across the ocean, to Paris, warrants the hazard of an ice field below." Besides which, of course, the thrill of that ice field, the thought of those bumps, tauten the nerves and are themselves a pleasure . . . and the same is true of mountaineering, diving, cave-exploring, gliding, and the rest.

The Lure of Physical Pleasure

Physical pleasure is too loudly advertised in these days to need a megaphone from me. Usually it stems from a skill, which may have to be painfully acquired. The rock or ice climber glides upward with a smooth motion which to the inexpert remains a miracle. And for all the frustrations of rock climbing, I know of few moments more precious than those in which I have stood poised on a ledge, master of my next upward move as of the view down; or in which I have felt that electrical comradeship that being roped together on a difficult climb with another person can give. Here is Gaston Rebuffat, the French guide, who climbed all of the six great north faces in the Alps and wrote what is almost a hymn to his profession about them.

We found ourselves climbing with ease and pleasure. Our movements were linked in smooth rhythm, like water flowing from a spring. All skills have this effect on a well trained body. . . . Thus the whole climb was pure joy, for, while superficially watching over the actual ascent, the spirit had leisure to wander happily. It was an exquisite afternoon; no incident marred the day.†

That was no easy climb but rather the north face of the Dru, above Chamonix, which he climbed with a friend in record time. Technique and fitness are such that the hands move almost inevitably to their holds, as if these were made for them and ready to their use.

As the climber mounts upward, so the diver glides down, in what must be one of the most pleasurable of all rhythms. Here, too, there is a technique, which is by now so much accepted that we forget the struggles, as well as the excite-

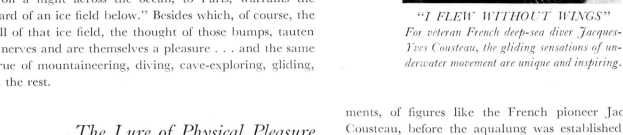

"I FLEW WITHOUT WINGS"
For veteran French deep-sea diver Jacques-Yves Cousteau, the gliding sensations of underwater movement are unique and inspiring.

ments, of figures like the French pioneer Jacques-Yves Cousteau, before the aqualung was established.

To halt and hang attached to nothing, no lines or air pipe to the surface, was a dream. At night I often had visions of flying by extending my arms as wings. Now I flew without wings.*

The dream of Leonardo fulfilled—in another element!

Other divers are more specific about the pleasure they get from this new freedom of movement. Hans Hass, the explorer of the Red Sea, writes:

If I wanted to make an upward leap of five metres, I simply gave myself a little push up and there I was. If I wanted to descend ten metres, I simply bent forward and glided down like a bird. I never got so near to a third-dimensional life as I did in this wreck, where every ladder and door provoked comparison with those of a normal vessel. No bird, however cleverly it might wing its way through the rigging, could surpass me. For in my case gravity did not count at all. I could glide in whatever way and in whatever direction I chose, and I could with equal ease remain perfectly motionless in space.†

I have the feeling that we are at present in the golden age of this type of diving; for it is still a comparatively recent discovery, to be sung lyrically, and not yet at the mercy of machine or commerce.

All these sensations add up to a supreme sense of well-being, which comes to some people in the most unlikely places. Isabella Bird was a frail little Englishwoman of the last century. She was short, with a disease of the spine that made her, at home, a semi-invalid. She wore a brace and seldom rose before midday. Then she was sent traveling for her health. At Hawaii she began to feel better and went climbing. In the Rocky Mountains she took on the tough life of a ranch with enthusiasm and climbed 14,000-foot

* The Spirit of St. Louis, by Charles A. Lindbergh (Scribner's, 1957).
† Starlight and Storm, by Gaston Rebuffat (Dutton, 1957).

* The Silent World, by Jacques-Yves Cousteau and Frédéric Dumas (Harper, 1953).
† Manta: Under the Red Sea, by Hans Hass (Rand McNally, 1953).

Longs Peak into the bargain. Off to Malaya she went, where she forded the Perak River half-submerged on an elephant. Later, finding herself on the point of marriage, she packed her boxes for Japan, where she lived among the Hairy Ainu of Hokkaido. Back home she bought a tricycle, but was off to Morocco before she could use it. When she died, at seventy-two, her boxes stood ready packed for China. I know of no more remarkable instance of the beneficial effects of adventure on the health.

The Lures of Companionship and Solitude

For some, the company of friends is a strong call to adventure; for others, the lure is the promise of solitude. For an example of the former I turn again to polar exploration, where the bond of hardship shows clearest. The Winter Journey of 1911 was a nightmare of five weeks, as we have seen. But it was undertaken by three friends.

In civilization men are taken at their own valuation because there are so many ways of concealment, and there is so little time, perhaps even so little understanding. These two men [Edward Wilson and H. R. Bowers] went through the Winter Journey and lived; later they went through the Polar Journey and died. They were gold, pure, shining, unalloyed. Words cannot express how good their companionship was. . . .

I am not going to pretend that this was anything but a ghastly journey, made bearable and even pleasant to look back upon by the qualities of my two companions who have gone.*

The gold of companionship! It is strange to what extremes of difficulty and danger a man will go to find it.

In the same vein the great French author and flier, Saint-Exupéry, exclaims:

Happiness! It is useless to seek it elsewhere than in this warmth of human relations. Our sordid interests imprison us within their walls. Only a comrade can grasp us by the hand and haul us free.

And these human relations must be created. One must go through an apprenticeship to learn the job. Games and risk are a help here. When we exchange manly handshakes, compete in races, join together to save one of us who is in trouble, cry aloud for help in the hour of danger—only then do we learn that we are not alone on earth.†

Solitude as a motive is not so easy to understand. Yet some people, as odd as they may be thought by the majority, approach the central experience better alone. My example of the "deepening" process and its effect is not taken from mountaineering, but from a profoundly wise man, William James, who once passed the night alone on Mount Marcy.

I spent a good deal of it in the woods, where the streaming moonlight lit up things in a magical checkered play. . . . The intense significance of some sort, of the whole scene, if only one could *tell* the significance; the intense inhuman remoteness of its inner life, and yet the intense *appeal* of it; its everlasting freshness and its immemorial antiquity and decay. . . . I can't find a single word for that significance, and I don't know what it was significant of, so there it remains, a mere boulder of impression.*

Alone or in company many people react almost magnetically to certain types of scene. Sometimes they prefer to penetrate it alone, sometimes in company. Whichever way it is, when they are there, the beauty of that scene fascinates them: it may be desert, a waste of snow, a shining peak, a broad sea. When they are home they dream of it until it lures them back. To each the dream is different, and equally compelling. I have often dreamed of mountains but am indifferent to the gray sea. Yet I know of men who, having stood once upon a coral sea bottom, have been so entranced that they have given up their lives from that moment to undersea exploration. To each his taste, and thank heaven the taste of each is different!

The Lure of Escape

The more anyone reads the story of others' adventures and contemplates his own, the more he must be struck with the frequency of the escape motive. In modern life there is a growing dichotomy: on the one side pressing claims from the complications of "civilized" existence, on the other a different world which, unless a man be scientific, becomes more and more divorced from the so-called realities of that earlier and humdrum life. What has surprised me is the formidable *number* of those who have first been moved to adventure by the plain longing to throw up office desk or classroom, factory or parade ground, and then gone on from there.

Undersea diving seems to me a perfect form of temporary escape, because the diver, wandering peacefully through a new element, enjoys a smooth mastery such as he can never achieve in "real" life. I was, therefore, delighted when I found an aqualung diver writing:

I have travelled to another world in which action is sister to the dream. I have swept away in the heart of the sea, at a depth of several fathoms, all my anxieties as a man. Worries of the moment, scientific curiosity, metaphysical doubts have all been hurled into the sea and I do not regret any of them.

Like many others I do not feel in perfect harmony with our age and the solitude of diving lulls and stays a deep-rooted dis-

CONTINUED ON PAGE 135

* The Worst Journey in the World
† Wind, Sand and Stars, by Antoine de Saint-Exupéry (Harcourt, Brace, 1949).

* A letter to his wife, quoted in An Experiment in Depth, by P. W. Martin (Pantheon, 1955).

"I TRIED TO REALIZE THAT AFTER 23 YEARS . . . I HAD SUCCEEDED" To Robert Peary, Arctic expeditions were his duty to his country. In 1909, after eight tries, he planted the American flag at the North Pole.

The Golden Age of the Dutch Republic

By C. V. WEDGWOOD

n a narrow, low-lying strip of coastal country in northern Europe, scarcely two hundred miles long—a country so water-logged that enemies and rivals spoke of it as a mud flat—there arose in the seventeenth century one of the great civilizations of the world. The Golden Age of the Dutch Republic stands out as one of the most comprehensive, most astonishing, and most admirable achievements of mankind, a monument alike to human industry and the human spirit.

From this little country, with its windy sand dunes and its damp pastures, ships went out to sail the farthest seas. On the mud flats large, solid, prosperous cities came into being. Their quays received the goods of all the world, which their merchants exchanged and distributed again to all the world. Their great banking houses financed the sovereigns of Europe. Thanks to its geographical position and the enterprise and energy of its people, the Dutch Republic was—only two generations after its founding—the richest commercial community Europe had yet seen.

Such a civilization, built on trade and industry, on hard work and financial acumen, might have been wholly materialist in all its manifestations. The Golden Age of the Dutch Republic might have been a golden age only in the narrowest and hardest sense. It was not so. This mercantile people, with their code of self-reliance and hard work, of enterprise, courage, and good craftsmanship, gave much more to the world than mere material gain. Scientists, thinkers, and poets flourished among them. The works of their great painters, luminous, tranquil, and profound, shine out among us still. Spiritual and material greatness were deeply, inextricably interwoven in the great achievement of the Dutch.

No precise bounds can be set to the epoch of their glory, but the generation from 1625 to 1648, during which Frederick Henry, Prince of Orange, guided their affairs, is usually taken as the high noon of the Golden Age. Rembrandt was painting, Frans Hals was at the height of his powers, Hugo Grotius was laying down the foundations of international law, Vondel was composing his great poetic dramas, Abel Tasman was exploring the far Pacific, and the great Dutch admirals Piet Heyn and Martin Tromp were sweeping the Spaniards off the seas. But this golden summer had already been preceded by a wonderfully promising spring and was to be followed by a fruitful autumn. The last of the harvest was not gathered until the end of the century.

Frederick Henry, Prince of Orange-Nassau, was stadholder of the Dutch Republic during its golden age. A brave general and able statesman, he was the third prince of his house (after William the Silent, his father, and Maurice, his brother) to lead the Dutch struggle for independence. Here, wearing the fine clothes he loved and riding his favorite gray charger, he appears before the fortress town of Maastricht, which he captured from the Spanish after a siege of four months in August, 1632. The painting is by Paulus van Hillegaert.

TEXT CONTINUED ON PAGE 18

15

*F*or *an afternoon of sport the solid families of The Hague liked to strap on their curly-toed skates and glide around the Vijver-berg, an artificial pond in the center of town. In this painting by Adam van Breen, Prince Maurice of Orange-Nassau and his party have come to watch the fun. Maurice, who ruled the United*

Netherlands as stadholder from 1587 to 1625, is the second figure to the left of the company of halberdiers. The title of stadholder, taken over from Spanish rule and conferred upon his reluctant father, William the Silent, became quasi-hereditary when it passed to Maurice and then to his younger brother Frederick Henry.

17

The Surrender of Breda *by Velazquez depicts a defeat suffered by Dutch arms in the year that Frederick Henry assumed rule. The blue-green distances of the watery Netherlands are seen between the forbidding uprights of the lances held by Spanish soldiers; in front of them, Spinola, the great Genoese soldier who fought for Spain, leans graciously forward to receive the keys of the town from Justin of Nassau, illegitimate son of William the Silent. Because it is so great a historic painting, this work by the Spanish court painter has made famous an event which was in fact only a local setback in the triumphant rise of the young Dutch Republic.*

TEXT CONTINUED FROM PAGE 15

The political story of the free and independent Dutch had begun a hundred years earlier. The Netherlands had come by a series of dynastic marriages to form a part of the great Hapsburg dominions, and in 1555 they were assigned to King Philip II of Spain as his share in the family inheritance. At that time the Reformation had shaken and divided Europe, and Philip II saw it as his mission to re-unite Europe within the fold of the Roman Catholic Church under the dominating influence of Spain. The Netherlands were to play an important part in his design, partly because of their strategic position at the mouth of the Rhine and opposite the English coast, and partly because of the great wealth of the southern Netherlands with their prosperous trading cities and their great port of Antwerp.

It was unfortunate for Philip's projects that the Protestant religion in various forms had already penetrated into the

18

Netherlands. His attempts to stamp it out, combined with an interfering economic policy, brought the country to the verge of revolt. At this, in 1567, he sent the Duke of Alva to impose an iron military rule on the recalcitrant people. But the Netherlanders found a leader in one of their noblemen, the Prince of Orange, William of Nassau—or William the Silent as he came to be called. Organizing a rebellion with heroic tenacity and against fearful odds, he succeeded in dislodging the Spaniards from the northern half of the country. He had hoped to liberate and to hold united the whole of the Netherlands, but after his assassination in 1584 it became clear that the rich southern provinces, which were Catholic in sympathy, would remain with Spain, while the northern regions alone would form the new and independent Dutch Republic.

Gradually this small new nation was recognized by surrounding European powers. It was a federated republic governed by elected representatives, although two sons of William the Silent in turn held the highest offices in the state, both civil and military. Prince Maurice, the elder son, was a soldier of formidable intelligence who fought the Spaniards to a standstill and made a twelve years' truce with them in 1609. He died in 1625, shortly after the resumption of the war. The rule of his brother Frederick Henry, which was later to be so fruitful and so glorious, began inauspiciously with the loss of the border fortress of Breda. Velazquez, court painter at Madrid, immortalized the surrender in one of his greatest pictures.

The capture of Breda was the last significant Spanish victory over the Dutch. Frederick Henry, the new Dutch leader, was not a military genius like his elder brother, but he had great tenacity and great patience, and he had inherited from his famous father, William the Silent, an inspiring capacity for remaining calm in the face of disaster. As a statesman he was to show himself, at least during his first and best years, just, tolerant, and wise; in external politics he was a persuasive and often subtle diplomat. He did not cause the Golden Age of Holland, but it is impossible to imagine it without his generous and reassuring presence in the background. Under his leadership the Dutch soon re-established equilibrium in the war with Spain and pushed doggedly on to final victory at the Peace of Münster in 1648. During all these years Spain was visibly a declining power, while the young Dutch Republic went from strength to strength.

From the very outset of the war of liberation, sea power had been of the first importance to the Dutch. There were two reasons for this: first, they had to prevent the Spanish fleet from feeding the battle front in the southern Netherlands with sea-borne reinforcements of men and arms and money; secondly, they had to keep open the channels of trade into their own country. They had built their prosperity on overseas trade and in particular on the herring industry; their fisheries were the basis of a great commerce in salt fish, a universal part of diet in an age when there was no canned food.

The Dutch now extended their trading ventures with increasing boldness, fiercely competing with other nations. Thus, early in the seventeenth century, Sir Walter Raleigh warned the English that they were losing ground in the northern waters. "We had a great trade in Russia seventy years," he asserted, "and about fourteen years past we sent store of goodly ships to trade in those parts, and three years past we sent out but four and this last year two or three; but to the contrary the Hollanders about twenty years since traded thither with two ships only, yet now they are increased to about thirty or forty, and one of their ships is as great as two of ours."

Dutch expansion was not confined to northern seas. Their ships boldly entered the enclosed waters of the Mediterranean and established commercial contact with Constantinople. With splendid daring they challenged the power of Spain on remoter seas in the West Indies, and sent out expeditions to find a northeastern or a northwestern passage to the treasures of the East. The survivors of one such expedition led by Willem Barents in 1595 came back with fearful stories of an Arctic winter spent on Novaya Zemlya. Henry Hudson, the English leader of another Dutch expedition in search of a northwest passage, sailed up the unknown majestic river which now bears his name and anchored off Manhattan island where soon the Dutch settlement of New Amsterdam would arise. Dutch navigators scattered their names over the map of the world; Cape Horn was named by Willem Schouten, who rounded it in 1616, after the little Dutch town of Hoorn, where he had been born. Abel Tasman, who in 1642 established the fact that Australia was an island, is commemorated in the name of Tasmania. But the energy and ambition of Dutch traders centered on the East Indies.

In 1595 Cornelis de Houtman sailed for the East Indies, returning two and a half years later from Java, to set all the church bells in Amsterdam ringing for joy of his arrival, laden with the spices of the East. It was the beginning of the Dutch East Indian empire. In 1602 the Dutch East India Company was founded, which competed ruthlessly with its English rival. Java, with its capital at Batavia, became the center of Dutch power in the East. They drove their English rivals out of the Malay Archipelago; they thrust the Portuguese out of Ceylon; they made themselves a foothold in Formosa. In energy and daring, in single-minded enterprise, they had not their equals; and the small country far off in Europe grew rich and confident as Dutch seamen and Dutch merchants took toll of the whole world.

The young, energetic people were proud of their mounting achievements. Books were written about them, pictures painted. The journeys of explorers were celebrated in poetry and carefully recorded in prose. The profit and glory of

*P*iet Heyn was commanding the navy of the West India Company when he captured the Spanish treasure fleet and thus established Dutch naval power. As reward he was made lieutenant admiral of Holland.

Dutch merchants was the perennial subject for painters, commissioned to paint portraits that were often set against the background of some Eastern scene, or showed in the distance some splendid ship unloading at the quay. The Dutch East Indiamen were the largest vessels afloat, palatial monsters of the high seas, armed against pirates and storms.

The English were rivals for the herring fisheries and competitors in the East Indian trade, but the Spaniards were still the principal enemy. Themselves a great seafaring nation and pioneers in exploration, it was long before they could bring themselves to realize that the Dutch had outdistanced them. But in 1628 Piet Heyn, veteran Dutch admiral and daring seaman, who had long harried the Spaniards in the West Indies, intercepted the Spanish treasure fleet off Cuba and destroyed it in the Bay of Matanzas. The booty that he brought home to Holland from the wrecked and captured Spanish vessels amounted in silver ore and goods to the value of eleven and a half million Dutch florins; its effect on the Netherlands' prosperity may be gathered from the fact that in that year the shareholders of the Dutch West India Company, which had financed Heyn's expedition, received a dividend of 50 per cent.

Such a loss, financial as well as naval, was crippling to Spain. Eleven years later, in 1639, the Dutch admiral Martin Tromp almost wholly destroyed, off the English coast, a Spanish fleet of seventy-seven vessels, an armada bringing troops and arms to prosecute the war in the Netherlands. From this second blow the staggering Spanish fortunes never recovered.

Dutch merchants consolidated the position prepared for them by Dutch explorers and Dutch admirals. In 1629 the burghers of Amsterdam declared with pride: "Through our economic management and exertions we have sailed all other nations off the seas, drawn almost all trade from other lands hither and served the whole of Europe with our ships." The statement was hardly an exaggeration. Besides their ancient trade in fish and their new expansion to the Indies, the Dutch had made themselves the intermediaries and the carriers for all Europe. The banks of Amsterdam now financed private and public enterprise far beyond the borders of Holland; the granaries of Amsterdam received corn brought from other countries in Dutch vessels and redistributed it through western Europe. Even the Spanish government had to turn a blind eye to the Dutch grain ships in their ports, without which people would have starved.

Once Antwerp in the Spanish Netherlands had been the financial center of the Western world and the greatest port in northern Europe. But Amsterdam took her trade and her pre-eminence from her. As early as 1619 an English traveler wrote, not without anxious envy, that Amsterdam, once a small fishing village, had "come in a short revolution of time by a monstrous increase of commerce and navigation to be one of the greatest marts in Europe."

The citizens of the young, expanding city behaved with unusual vision. Instead of leaving its growth to chance, they evolved in 1612 one of the earliest and most enlightened town-planning schemes in Europe. The expansion of Amsterdam has truly been called a "triumph of communal co-operation," for the scheme that was laid down by a highly intelligent committee was obediently put into effect by succeeding generations of citizens. The plan was in essence simple: a series of concentric canals, the three *Grachten*, were to contain the city. They were planned spaciously, like three great horseshoes one inside the other, and it was believed that allowance had been made for the utmost development of the city. In fact the plan fulfilled the needs of Amsterdam for over two hundred years, and few town planners in our own time would hope for better success.

Although Amsterdam towered in importance over all the Dutch cities, all shared in the prosperity of the age and each had its proper civic pride. With the change of religion, the ancient Gothic churches of the older towns had been strenuously cleared of "idolatrous" images, but the structures were carefully preserved. The severely whitewashed interiors of these lofty buildings have been recorded by many a painter of the seventeenth century, often with a black-gowned Calvinist preacher in the pulpit and a full congregation of burghers and their wives intently listening.

The greatest age of church decoration had gone by, and the Calvinist religion in general imposed austerity. But national or civic pride now and again asserted itself. William the Silent, the Liberator, the Father of the Fatherland, could not go uncommemorated, and his rich Italianate tomb, with marble columns and bronze figures, stands out in startling contrast to the severe simplicity of the Gothic church in Delft where it is housed.

The buildings of ancient convents and monasteries were also usually preserved. Some of them were transformed into the residences of the rich, like the convent at Delft where William the Silent made his home. Others were used as civic buildings; still others were turned into orphanages or homes for the aged. The Dutch cities prided themselves on the orderly if sometimes rather authoritative benevolence that kept their streets free of beggars. The occasional appearance of a beggar in street scenes painted by Dutch artists suggests that they were not quite uniformly successful, but we have the contemporary evidence of travelers that it was a rare thing to see a beggar among the Dutch—and this at a time when most great cities teemed with them.

Deserted and orphan children were brought together into institutions and carefully educated to be respectable citizens. Old and disabled soldiers were regularly pensioned—a system that scarcely existed in any other country at this time. The aged poor were gathered together and decently cared for in almshouses. Frans Hals, the great painter, who fell on evil days, spent much of his time in later years in one of these at Haarlem, which today houses a museum containing the last pictures that he painted, portrait groups of the governors of the almshouse.

From energy and industry had come great wealth, and the Dutch merchants, both in their civic and their private lives, showed an orderly discrimination in the uses to which they put their money. Although three great noblemen, the Princes of Orange, remained for many years at the head of the state, and the small, exclusive group of Dutch nobility preserved their existence and their identity as a class, the whole tone of the young republic was that of the mercantile middle class. It was their wealth and vigor, their aspirations

The Spanish Silver Fleet, laden with the treasure of New Spain, was starting its annual voyage home when Piet Heyn fell upon it off Cuba in 1628. He captured some of the ships at sea, ran the rest to ground in Matanzas Bay. The Dutch West India Company got the prize, while the Dutch nation got revenge for all the years of Spanish rule.

and prejudices which gave force and direction to every part of the national life.

How came it that this civilization of hard-headed, hard-working merchants, adventurers, industrialists, dairy farmers, and seamen inspired great literature, great thought, and even greater painting? What made this mercantile society, in the words of the modern Dutch historian Pieter Geyl, "so abundant, so free, so receptive?" The secret lies, paradoxically almost, in the Dutch religion. The Calvinists had formed the spearhead of the revolt against Spain, and they remained dominant in the young republic. Calvinism is not a religion that greatly encourages freedom of speculation or, for that matter, aesthetic sensibility. But these people had fought for freedom of conscience for themselves and were therefore committed to it. The Calvinist Dutch might bitterly disapprove of other religious doctrines; they might curtail the civil and political power of those who held them, but they could not deny them the right to worship and believe as they chose. Moreover, quite apart from the principle of religious liberty for which they had fought, the Dutch could not, for practical reasons, do without the industry and skill of the religious minorities. There remained always within the Republic a considerable Roman Catholic minority who had never changed their faith; there was, especially in Amsterdam, a large and growing Jewish community; and Protestant refugees of many different sects continuously flooded in from all parts of Europe. The work and co-operation of all these were needed by the young republic, and the existence of so many different communities within a small country naturally stimulated the circulation of ideas.

Religious conflict was by no means at an end. There was constant jealousy and fear of the Roman Catholic minority, and there was from time to time harsh conflict between Protestant groups which broke out in violence. A bitter struggle during the years of truce with Spain had ended only when Prince Maurice made himself virtually—for a space—dictator. But this very friction stimulated the growth of ideas and generated new energy. Indeed the extraordinary vitality of Dutch culture at this epoch may well have been an outcome of the tension between the new and the old, the experimental and the conventional.

A mercantile community, to be successful, as the Dutch so transcendently were at this time, must encourage not only self-reliance and industry among its members but also originality and enterprise. No one can accuse the Dutch merchants of the Golden Age of being hidebound or conventional in their business operations. Here they showed courage and imagination. In politics, in religion, in the arts, they might be—and probably most of them were—

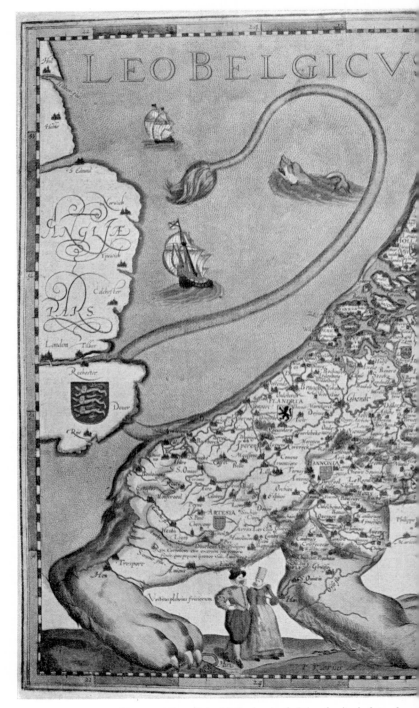

The proud lion of the Netherlands, fighting for its independence from Spain, roars defiance at the Continent, while flicking its tail toward England. This marvelously imaginative map of the United Provinces was engraved at Amsterdam in 1617 by Pieter

extremely conventional. But in such a society, where courage, originality, and enterprise are encouraged because of their value in business, there will always be a considerable number of men and women in whom these same valuable qualities will be directed to quite different ends—to scientific enquiry, to philosophic speculation, to art or literature. Some of these may come into conflict with the community; others will find a way of being accepted. A vigorous mercantile community can thus provide the artist and the

FROM *Decorative Printed Maps of the 15th to 18th Centuries;* BY PERMISSION OF THE BRITISH MUSEUM, COURTESY STAPLES PRESS LIMITED, LONDON

*an den Keere. In map making, as in politics, it marks a notable
Dutch achievement. During the seventeenth century the studios of
Hondius, Jansson, Blaeu, and others at Amsterdam turned out,
of seamen and merchants, the most decorative maps ever produced.*

the Silent had been the foundation of the first
Dutch university, at Leiden in 1575, when only a
small part of the country had been liberated and
the war was still in a critical stage. In the ensuing
fifty years, provinces had vied with each other in the
encouragement of learning, and universities had been
founded at Groningen, Utrecht, and Harderwijk.
These universities were seats of learning where a fine
tradition of scholarship was steadily built up, but
they were often the scene of violent disputes between
traditional teaching and new ideas. At Utrecht the
theories of Galileo were vehemently opposed, as were
also those of the French scientist and philosopher Descartes. The professor of medicine was required to
teach only such doctrine as had been laid down by
the ancients. Doubts were felt as to whether the theory
that the blood circulated in the body, as the Englishman Harvey had recently argued, could be reconciled
with the Scriptures. As late as 1642 the Senate of
Utrecht passed a resolution against the new scientific
teaching which was making converts among the
younger professors. "It is contrary to the ancient philosophy which the universities of the whole world have
thus far taught with wise deliberation," they said, and
added a warning that "there may be deduced from
it by inexperienced youth several false and prepos-
terous notions which conflict with the other sciences
and faculties and above all with the orthodox religion."

Yet the country whose academic teachers passed
this resolution counted among its citizens some of the
greatest pioneers of modern science. Anton van Leeuwenhoek, combining immense technical dexterity with
concentrated powers of observation, first greatly improved the magnifying powers of the microscope and
then used it to penetrate secrets of nature. He was
the first to describe accurately blood corpuscles and
to discern bacteria. His contemporary, Jan Swammer-
dam, who also, in a way which seems to have been
peculiarly Dutch, combined great technical skill with
an inquiring and patient observation, studied the
anatomy of invertebrates and was the first fully to observe (and most delicately to illustrate) the transforma-
tion of insects. He watched and recorded the process by
which a caterpillar becomes a butterfly and the frog
emerges from the tadpole. But both these men were,
in the modern sense, amateurs: they worked outside the
universities, discussing their ideas with like-minded friends
and exchanging discoveries and information with other
interested experimenters in different walks of life.

In spite of some academic opposition, the atmosphere of
educated Dutch society was sympathetic and stimulating to
men with new ideas. Whatever the pundits of Utrecht might
say, it was in the congenial atmosphere of Holland that the
greatest of all the new philosophers, the Frenchman René

thinker with that mixture of encouragement and frustration,
of opposition and of stimulation, in which many talents
flower. The Renaissance culture of the Italian cities had
had something of this in it; the pattern can be detected in
such great and prosperous societies as England in the nineteenth century or the United States in the twentieth. It
was evident in seventeenth-century Holland.

The contrast and the challenge is seen at its clearest in
the world of learning. One of the first acts of William

23

Descartes, lived his happiest years and wrote his *Discours de la Methode*, long to be regarded as the foundation of modern philosophy.

In the field of political philosophy the Dutch themselves can claim Hugo Grotius as one of the greatest pioneers of modern thought. His epoch-making book *De Jure Belli et Pacis* laid the foundations of international law. But he wrote it in exile, in France. Here was an odd paradox, that the Dutch Republic, which gave asylum to religious refugees and men of learning from all over Europe, forced one of its greatest thinkers to seek safety outside its borders. It was not, however, on account of his opinions that Grotius fled the country, but because he was one of the victims involved in the political crisis at the end of Prince Maurice's rule.

Dutch literature of the seventeenth century reflects the same conflicting tendencies. This young independent people had a language and a way of thought very much their own. But their past history had made them also conscious of a position in Western Europe; they could not sever the links that still bound them to the southern Spanish Netherlands from which they had so recently separated themselves. The culture of the South was the international culture of late Renaissance Europe: its greatest painter was Peter Paul Rubens, its poets and writers belonged to the wide and rich tradition common to such princely and aristocratic lands as France, Spain, and contemporary Italy. But in the Dutch Republic—geographically so near, politically so different—international influences and the strong individual flavor of the new mercantile republic were strangely and often attractively mingled.

The most famous poets of the time present a study in contrasts. There was Constantijn Huygens, a man of wide culture and learning, a diplomat well versed in European society, whose poems have all the mannered subtlety of the cultivated poets of the earlier seventeenth century in England, in France, in Germany, or in Spain. He admired and translated John Donne with a rare skill. A younger man, Joost van den Vondel, has often been compared to Milton, not merely because one of his greatest works was the poetic drama *Lucifer*. He managed, with a ravishing fluency, to capture in Dutch (which is not the easiest of languages for poetry) the subtlety and ripeness of baroque culture.

In sharp contrast is the work of Jacob Cats, who celebrated in anecdotal, didactic verse the domestic joys and duties, the morality and prejudices of contemporary Dutch civilization. His popular fame was, and remained, enormous; his works were, next to the Bible, the literature best known to the Dutch people for centuries. He was the people's poet par excellence and was familiarly thought of as "Father Cats." But he owed his permanent position in literature to more remarkable qualities. He illuminated his conventional opinions with much genuine wisdom and with an understanding of men and women, in the daily problems of life, which is both humorous and humane.

*T*he return of Cornelis de Houtman's ship from the Indies in 1597 (painted by H. C. Vroom) signalized the opening of the East Indies trade. This great enterprise, the chief source of the Netherlands' wealth, was carried on in huge, towering East Indiamen, built successfully to outrun the Spanish and outcarry the English. At the peak of its prosperity, the Dutch East India Company counted in its possession 150 trading ships, 40 ships of war, and 10,000 soldiers.

*I*n the painting at left, a Dutch trader in the Indies points with pride to his ships in the Dutch-built port of Batavia. The burghers and their wives took readily enough to the parasols and slave boys of the East, but they clung to their North European clothes beneath the southern sun.

*E*ast India House was the headquarters in Amsterdam of the Dutch trading empire. The East India Company not only enjoyed a monopoly of the Indies trade but exercised the powers of government, complete with laws and courts, over a vast watery empire extending from the Straits of Magellan to the Cape of Good Hope. During a period of 198 years its dividends averaged 18 per cent.

'T OOST INDISCH HUYS.

The most famous center of Dutch literary life during the Golden Age was the castle of Muiden on the Zuider Zee where Pieter Corneliszoon Hooft gathered about him a remarkable group of friends who, in the pleasant atmosphere of his country house, exchanged ideas, discussed each other's writings, made music, and followed the new theories and the new discoveries that seemed to flower almost daily in the brave new world. Hooft himself wrote a famous history of the recent wars with Spain, a work conceived in the classical manner and based on the style of Tacitus. The circle included also Constantijn Huygens; occasionally Joost van den Vondel; the famous scholar Gerard Vossius; Laurens Reaal, soldier, seaman, and poet; Samuel Coster, who was both a physician and a dramatist; and the two sister poetesses, both women of exceptional charm, Anna and Maria Visscher.

Women were not excluded from the culture of the Dutch Golden Age. Indeed they could hardly have been, for it is one of the characteristics of a hard-working mercantile society that the woman is expected to show energy, industry, and intelligence in the management of her household, and sometimes to take a part in her husband's business. Moreover, a seafaring people, whose menfolk are often absent for long periods, will naturally delegate responsibility to their women. There was, of course, no question of equality; it is clear from the poems of Cats (and indeed from the whole domestic morality of Calvinism) that the woman's place was one of obedience to the man, but it was none the less a recognized and valuable place. The Dutch woman was not brought up to be a voiceless drudge nor, in a higher class of society, to be merely decorative. She was brought up to be an intelligent and valued, if junior, partner in a man's world.

It was natural therefore that a few women at least should make their mark in the world of learning and the arts. The most famous of them was Anna Maria van Schuurman, who was famous rather for the multiplicity of her talents than

A SHARP VIEW OF THE DUTCH

BY SIR WILLIAM TEMPLE
BRITISH AMBASSADOR TO HOLLAND,
1668

The merchants and tradesmen are of mighty industry. Never any country traded so much and consumed so little. They buy infinitely, but 'tis to sell again. They are the great masters of Indian spices and Persian silks, but wear plain woolen and feed upon their own fish and roots. They sell the finest of their own cloth to France and buy coarse out of England for their own wear. They send abroad the best of their own butter and buy the cheapest out of Ireland for their own use. They furnish infinite luxury which they never practice, and traffic in pleasure which they never taste.

Their common riches lie in everyman's spending less than he has coming in.

All appetites and passions seem to run lower and cooler here than in other countries, avarice excepted. Their tempers are not airy enough for joy, nor warm enough for love. This is talked of sometimes among the younger men, but as a thing they have heard of, rather than felt. I have known some that impersonated lovers well enough, but none that I ever thought were at heart in love.

Holland is a country where the earth is better than the air, and profit more in request than honor, where there is more sense than wit, more good nature than good humor and more wealth than pleasure. Where a man would choose rather to travel than to live, shall find more things to observe than desire and more persons to esteem than to love.

for her supreme excellence in any one field. She was an artist of distinction, a linguist, scholar, and theologian, who corresponded with some of the most learned men of her time. Among the painters, the most famous was Judith Leyster, one of whose most striking pictures, *The Lute Player*, was for a long time thought to be the work of Frans Hals.

When we think of the Golden Age of the Dutch Republic we think above all of the great painters. A wonderful series of canvases from many different hands have recorded both the outward face and the inward spirit of that great epoch. Such landscape painters as Philips de Koninck, Jacob van Ruisdael, Jan van Goyen, and Aart van der Neer have recorded the physical appearance of their country at this time. We can see, in every detail, the farmsteads with their red-tiled roofs, the water mills and the windmills, the wide flat fields over which the windy clouds make moving patterns of sun and shade, the winding canals, the neat little towns with their towers and spires seen across pastures where cattle graze. We can see the people who inhabited these fields and towns, about their everyday work and their holiday amusements. In the foreground of Ruisdael's *View of Haarlem* they are bleaching great strips of linen cloth in the sunny fields; Aelbert Cuyp and Paul Potter preferred to show them pasturing their fine dairy cattle. Jan van Goyen shows them sailing their canals or putting their ships out to sea; Wouwerman, when he is not painting battle scenes, has caught the atmosphere of salt and sand and wind on the dunes as the fishermen bring in their catch; Avercamp, Adriaen van der Venne, and Aart van der Neer liked to show them during the winter, skating and sleighing on their frozen canals.

Other painters preferred indoor scenes. Thanks to them we know more of the Dutch middle classes in their everyday setting than of any other people at this period. Gerard Terborch captures the moment of concentration as young people make music in a comfortable, well-appointed room;

*T*he real power in Holland lay not with the noble families but with the rich, solid burghers. This couple never knew how well they chose when they asked a young painter named Rembrandt to do their portrait. He must have pleased them with his careful attention to the fine texture of their stiff black clothes and the starched delicacy of their ruffs. Such men and women of substance created the first bourgeois state and thus set a social pattern for the Western world to follow.

Pieter de Hooch has shown them in the small gardens of their town houses, playing at skittles or taking a glass of wine in the quiet mellow afternoon; or, moving within doors, he catches the vista from some shadowed, tile-floored room where two young people sedately sit along the sun-streaked corridor with a distant glimpse of a serving maid or some gay, peeping child. Jan Steen, equally at home in the fresh air or the congested interior, has shown roistering parties of country folk dancing in the courtyard of an inn, or enjoying the fun of the fair, or family parties celebrating a christening or perhaps the feast of Saint Nicholas in some four-square, cheerfully overcrowded room. Certain characters in his pictures come in again and again—the kindly Granny, the funny, ugly little girl, the naughty grimacing boy. These are surely his own family, seen with love and humor, and the rooms must be those of his own home, for when he was not a painter he was a jolly innkeeper.

These painters of popular scenes flourished in response to a demand for a new kind of picture. In earlier times and in other countries painters had worked for the Church, for princes, or for wealthy private patrons. They had painted great religious subjects for altarpieces or had decorated the walls of palaces. But, apart from portraits and occasional traveling altarpieces painted for diplomats and princes, the demand for smaller paintings, for easel paintings, had been light. But the new Dutch middle class wanted homely paintings to decorate the walls of their comfortable rooms. They wanted secular paintings because they were predominantly Protestant, and they valued above all lifelike representations of their countryside, their domestic life, and the objects that gave them pleasure—great baskets of fruit and flowers or an arrangement of crystal goblets on a precious piece of oriental carpet. The demand for them made these paintings into an investment; especially good examples changed hands for high prices, and even quite humble Dutch burghers and Dutch farmers thought it not only a pleasant thing in itself to buy paintings, but a good speculation. John Evelyn, the English diarist, thus describes a Dutch picture market at Rotterdam in 1641:

"We arrived late at Rotterdam where was their annual mart or fair, so furnished with pictures (especially landscapes and drolleries) that I was amazed. Some I bought and sent into England. The reason for this store of pictures and their cheapness proceeds from their want of land to employ their stock, so that it is an ordinary thing to find a common farmer lay out two or three thousand pounds in this commodity. Their houses are full of them, and they vend them at the fairs to very great gain."

There was a rising demand for portraits too, as the Dutch burghers gained in wealth and confidence and liked to hang on their walls paintings of themselves, their wives and children that captured not only a likeness but also fitly represented the social standing, the prosperity, and distinction of

TEXT CONTINUED ON PAGE 33

Anna Maria van Schuurman was the leading feminine light of Dutch intellectual and literary circles. Author, artist, philosopher, and mistress of twelve languages, she wrote a Latin dissertation on "The Aptitude of Woman's Mind for Science and Literature."

No way of life in all history has been preserved with such loving detail as that of seventeenth-century Holland. And of all the artists who devoted themselves to this meticulous record, Jan Vermeer of Delft was the true genius. This painting, The Artist in His Studio, *shows Vermeer himself at work in the room where he executed almost all—less than forty—of his paintings. Because he showed the back of his head, no one will ever know what Vermeer looked like. But here we see many of the things that appear in his other paintings—the tile floor, the brocade hangings, the wall map of the Netherlands, and the streaming light that he used to such radiant purpose. Vermeer's widow gave this painting to her mother, and in passing through various hands it lost its identity. In 1813 it sold for fifty florins as a Pieter de Hooch, but a century later Vermeer's fame had risen to such a level that Andrew Mellon supposedly bid $2,000,000 for it. Adolf Hitler got it for a while and hung it in his mountain chalet at Berchtesgaden. When the U.S. Third Army overran Austria in 1945 it found the painting hidden with the Nazi art treasure in a salt mine in the mountains above Salzburg. General Patton returned it to its owner, the state art museum at Vienna.*

"This is the Sunday of life," wrote Hegel of Dutch genre painting. No one loved to paint it better than Jan Steen, whose Merry Company *shows a family, full of good Dutch food and high spirits, ready for wine and music.*

Frans Hals, painter of youth and merriment, was brought to bankruptcy by the baker from whom he borrowed to feed his ten children. The city paid his rent, and his last commission came from the ladies who appear in this gray and somber portrait, The Women Guardians of the Haarlem Almshouse.

The Blue Girl by Cornelisz Verspronck was just the painting to appeal to a fond parental eye. The family-loving Dutch adored, indulged, and, in the opinion of foreigners, thoroughly spoiled their children. Visitors from France were scandalized to find the rosy Dutch youngsters talking back to their parents.

*A*nton van Leeuwenhoek, famous nat-
uralist, developed the microscope
and used it to penetrate many secrets of
nature, including bacteria, red blood corpuscles, and the cell structure of plants.

*H*ugo Grotius began his work in international law at Leiden in Holland but fell into political trouble with
the stadholder and fled to Paris, where he
wrote his classic De Jure Belli et Pacis.

*C*onstantijn Huygens, poet and diplomat, was the brightest literary
light of Holland for half a century.
His son, Christian, made an even greater
name in mathematics and astronomy.

TEXT CONTINUED FROM PAGE 28

the sitter. The clothes are usually somber, but the quality
of the stuff is carefully shown; black silk facings shine
against the deeper richness of black velvet—no easy trick
for a painter to catch the precise texture of the different
materials. A gleaming jewel, a gold chain, the snowy
contrast of a fine muslin ruff or a lace collar—these are the
principal ornaments, and for the artist often the only points
of color and excitement that he can use to emphasize his
composition. Dutch portrait painters acquired an extraordinary forcefulness in the treatment of the human face and
hands, and an extraordinary skill in working out a striking
design with small points of color and relief.

An easier task confronted the artist who was required
to paint one of the group paintings, which were also immensely in demand. Companies of merchants, learned
societies, and above all—for this was a country still at war—
the officers of the local volunteers wished to be painted in
groups. So there came into being the innumerable group
portraits of citizen-officers, wearing the broad, gold-fringed,
many-colored sashes which at that time were the designating
marks of military men. The only essential was that the face
of each man should be clearly shown.

Rembrandt gave offense by breaking this rule. Carried

*T*he Little Street *by Jan Vermeer radiates the
pride and joy which every Dutchman felt in his
home. Often built of red brick, a Dutchman's house
might be plain on the outside, but inside would be filled
with things of comfort and beauty to please his family.*

away by his own more profound and subtle vision of the
play of light and shade, he painted in *The Sortie of the
Banning Cocq Company* (familiarly and quite incorrectly
known as *The Night Watch*) one of the greatest of his pictures, and certainly the most memorable of all the group
portraits of this epoch. But it is easy to understand why some
of the sitters, whose forms and faces are lost in shadow, were
far from pleased with the result.

Rembrandt was for a time a fashionable and successful
portrait painter, but he stands apart from the portrait
painters and genre painters who supplied the new and
eager demands of the Dutch. He has the quality of genius
which (like that of Shakespeare in another sphere) is outside
historic time and place. But this can and should be said:
Rembrandt could have achieved the fulfillment of his
genius probably nowhere else so well as in seventeenth-
century Holland. Amsterdam with its world-wide trade
provided him with exciting and infinite visual material;
his book was life, and he read men and learned in the end to
set down what he had read with a sad and silent wisdom
that has never been equaled. In Amsterdam his penetrating
talent could draw on a multitude of different kinds of men
and women—the philosopher, the merchant, the soldier,
the rich young girl, the grizzled seaman, the kitchen maid,
or the withdrawn faces of rabbis.

For a time he was successful, but genius so individual
and so strong can rarely retain popular favor. He went
beyond his public and fell into disfavor. But he was never
utterly neglected. He always retained a small group of
discriminating admirers and of patrons who valued and

bought his pictures. It is the great merit of a society like that of seventeenth-century Holland—so competitive and so various—that it has room for small groups, literary and artistic cliques, which can sustain and encourage work outside the grasp of the general public.

It would not be strictly true to say that Rembrandt reveals the inner spirit of the Dutch at this time. He is a painter of the spirit, but his message is at the same time so individual and so universal that it would be a belittlement to attach it merely to the Dutch Golden Age. But no epoch, however fruitful, can be held to be truly great unless it has produced one giant of universal stature, one genius who transcends time and place. For the Golden Age of the Dutch Republic that giant is Rembrandt.

One other painter of this time has a claim to rank among the greatest—a painter whose achievement, unlike that of Rembrandt, belongs in time and space and by every outward convention to Holland in the seventeenth century and to no other epoch or place in the world. That painter is Jan Vermeer of Delft. He depicted with absolute faithfulness the domestic scenes and simple views that were so dear to Dutch collectors. A girl offers a glass of wine to a visitor; a housewife sits sewing in her doorway; a youthful party make music at the virginals; a young woman is discovered reading a love letter. The broom is propped against the wall, the paved floor has been mopped clean, the sun throws onto the dazzlingly white wall the harsh shadows of the heavy picture frames, picks up the sheen of a satin skirt, lingers in the soft glow of a pearl earring. It is the world of Gerard Terborch, of Jan Steen, and Pieter de Hooch. But it is also—and who can say why?—a moment stopped out of time. Here is an incident of no importance, a fragment from the lives of unknown people held forever, not just as a picture but as a reality. With the other Dutch genre painters we know we are looking at a picture; with Jan Vermeer we are experiencing a living moment.

With him, therefore, we come nearest to the inner essence of the Dutch seventeenth century. The zest for liberation, the adventurousness, the energy, and the wealth of this remarkable people do not explain all. Politically they achieved freedom; materially they achieved wealth; their Golden Age was built on these things, but they are not the spirit and the secret of its greatness. What else must there have been? Does the secret lie in this intensity of *living*, this concentration of the spirit, which Vermeer has so perfectly and so indefinably captured within the narrow limits of his few surviving paintings?

A leading interpreter of the seventeenth century, Miss C. V. Wedgwood is the author of such works as The Thirty Years' War, Oliver Cromwell, William the Silent, Richelieu and the French Monarchy, *and* Seventeenth Century Literature. *Her latest book,* The King's Peace, *on the Stuart period in her native Britain, is soon to be followed by* The King's War.

Coat of arms of Frederick Henry

*T*he apotheosis of Frederick Henry is the subject of this painting entitled Allegory of the Peace of Münster, *by Adriaen van Nieulandt. Frederick Henry had died in 1647, just too soon to see the culmination of his life's work in the Treaty of Münster, which brought a victorious end to the eighty-year struggle with Spain. In this splendidly baroque painting the Stadholder stands in a golden chariot, just to the right of the center of the canvas. Before him, with the Dutch lion beside her, sits the red-robed Spirit of the Netherlands; behind him ride Religion, Victory, and Liberty. The four figures drawing the chariot are Justice, Integrity, Magnanimity, and Prudence. At lower left, Juno, Mars, and Venus wait to receive the conquering hero. The bound figure in the foreground represents War, while the four gray-headed Tritons are the rivers Schelde, Maas, Rhine, and Y. Aloft, the allegorical figure of Abundance brings food to the devastated country, while cherubs bear the arms of the house of Orange-Nassau. Below Abundance, a white-robed Peace extends her right hand to a kneeling woman who clasps seven arrows to symbolize the seven United Provinces. With her other hand Peace presents an olive branch to Frederick Henry's son and heir, the young Prince William II of Orange-Nassau. Prince William had only three years to rule before he died of smallpox, but a week after he died, his widow gave birth to William III, who grew up to be not only stadholder of the Netherlands but, after the Glorious Revolution of 1688, king of England as well.*

A Memorandum

By WILLIAM HARLAN HALE

KLEMENS WENZEL NEPOMUK LOTHAR VON METTERNICH-WINNEBURG
1773-1859

AUSTRIAN STATESMAN AND DIPLOMAT
AMBASSADOR TO BERLIN AND PARIS
IMPERIAL MINISTER OF FOREIGN AFFAIRS, 1809-1848
IN 1813, CONCLUDED TREATY OF ALLIANCE WITH NAPOLEON
LATER IN SAME YEAR, CONCLUDED TREATY OF ALLIANCE AGAINST HIM
LEADING ARCHITECT OF THE EUROPEAN COALITION AGAINST FRANCE
CREATED HEREDITARY PRINCE OF THE AUSTRIAN EMPIRE
CHIEF ARBITER OF THE CONGRESS OF VIENNA, 1814-15
INSPIRER AND UPHOLDER OF THE HOLY ALLIANCE
LIFELONG DEFENDER OF ABSOLUTE MONARCHY AGAINST LIBERAL
IDEAS AND REVOLUTIONARY MOVEMENTS
FORCED TO SURRENDER OFFICE AND FLEE DURING
THE POPULAR UPRISINGS OF 1848

Esteemed colleague, I know that any communication between us may be suspect. My name is not popular in a country that still tends to look upon Old World diplomats as jaded intriguers. But then, my friend, neither is your name overly popular in European circles fearful of what they sometimes regard as New World moralists dancing upon the brink. You and I stand far apart in time, place, and method; yet I often feel we walk on common ground. For both of us have gone forth to mobilize great alliances against Revolution. Both have dueled with dictators at the summit. And both of us, for our pains, have been widely misunderstood. How paradoxical that you and I, who tried only to set seals of order and civilized posture upon our times, should both remain so . . . controversial.

Do you sometimes ask yourself why this should be, or is your age one in which a Foreign Minister's unpopularity is taken as a matter of course? You and I are international professionals in a world that seems to prefer the amateur spirit, and our problem is that of the artist whose full worth may not be recognized in his own time. For the marshaling of coalitions is the statesman's highest art, and the more diverse or improbable the coalition, the higher the art. In this I was virtually a Rembrandt, while as for you . . . history will tell.

I respect your coalition against Communism as a virtuous one. Mine against Napoleon was simpler: its aim was merely to survive. It won me a reputation for brilliance, whereas actually my genius lay simply in patience. I have often asked myself which is the more tedious—a rampant dictator or a reluctant ally. Like you, I had to rally the dull Prussians and the insular British, and many were the times when in my impatience I neared the point of threatening them with an "agonizing reappraisal"—although, to

From: Prince Klemens von Metternich

To: John Foster Dulles

Subject: The Art of Outstaying a Dictator

be sure, I did not say so publicly. In the end I prevailed because I left brilliance to Bonaparte, trusting that he would be betrayed by it, while I raised against him a force as seismic as it was slow. So beware of brilliance, good colleague: the future lies in outstaying it.

Let them outtalk you, even outshine you, but never isolate you. I feel sure you are a realist despite your strong evangelical tone. Even prayer, I find, is best in company. For my part—believe me—I was also a man of high principle whenever I could afford to be one, which was not as often as I would have liked.

I grant that in some respects your task is more difficult than mine ever was. How I feel for you when I read of your having to deal with Foreign Relations committees, Opposition busybodies, and the frequently critical Mr. James Reston of the New York *Times!* I had nothing like that in my time. As the first servant of my late, beloved Emperor Francis, whatever I told *our* leading newspaper correspondent (a gentleman named Gentz) to write, he wrote—and the Emperor sometimes even read. As the Crown's first Minister I was also its chief traveling diplomat, dealing on my own with the Corsican in his lair just as you yourself descend upon foreign potentates everywhere. But whereas I managed with only a handful of underlings, I see you have been saddled with a State Department establishment totaling over ten thousand—for what purpose I cannot tell. Wars and bureaucracies, what terrible scourges!

And you labor under another, severer handicap. Unlike your nation, the one I served was not mighty; it was merely fortunately placed. Austria, I sometimes think, was hardly more than a geographic incident in the history of the Hapsburg dynasty. But, flanked by the rival empires of Napoleon and Czar Alexander, it had the priceless advantage of standing in the middle—and arbitrating. Sometimes just a touch of pressure on my part sufficed to tilt the scales of Europe. Generals must lead from strength, but diplomats often do best in the absence of it and by turning others' strength to their own advantage. I, for one, never venerated generals sitting on their arsenals, so long as I myself was free to maneuver.

Your country's greatness, on the other hand, often forces you to take up fixed positions at one end of the scale, which both exalts and confines you. Immobility is something I would find most uncomfortable. Meanwhile, you are subject to the alternate temptation to embark on moral crusades as a substitute for bargaining, and this can become even more painful. In my day the idealistic young Czar Alexander wanted to mount just such a crusade to wipe out the remnants of Bonapartism, and I told him flatly I would have nothing to do with it. My own aims were simply the limited and unheroic ones of equilibrium and stability. Young Alexander went so far as to challenge me to a duel, but then thought better of it: he was not all that heroic. For, with a little guidance on my part from jaded Vienna, he saw that what he really needed was stability, too, in preference to massive retaliation.

I know I have been dismissed in modern times as an agent of the old absolutism. Yet the tyranny of the absolute sometimes reappears in the very places that say they have no use for it. I was free to rely on art; you now suffer under the monstrous rigidities of science. Still, I trust that you and the estimable American Republic will survive your Soviet antagonists just because they are more scientifically inclined than you, more single-minded, apparently better organized, and therefore more the prisoners of their own power.

Marlon Brando

THE CULT OF UNTHINK

By ROBERT BRUSTEIN

With heaves, grunts, pigment splotches, and howls, "cool" Beat Generation practitioners of the arts are indulging in self-expression of many sorts

When a hitherto unknown actor named Marlon Brando eleven years ago assumed the role of Stanley Kowalski, the glowering, inarticulate hero of Tennessee Williams' *A Streetcar Named Desire*, few people realized the symbolic importance of that creation. For Brando was to personify an entire postwar generation of troubled spirits trying to find an identity. Today we find his Kowalski wherever we look, whether in our latest literature, our poetry, our painting, our movies, our popular music, or on our city streets. In one guise or another he is the hero of the Beat Generation.

This new ideal image, as Brando first gave it dramatic form and as tribal followers from coast to coast have adopted it, is that of a man of much muscle and little mind, often surly and discontented, prepared to offer violence with little provocation. He peers out at the world from under beetling eyebrows, his right hand rests casually on his right hip. Walking with a slouching, shuffling gait, he scratches himself often and almost never smiles. He is especially identified by the sounds that issue from his mouth. He squeezes, he grunts, he passes his hand over his eyes and forehead, he stares steadily, he turns away, he scratches, then again faces his adversary, and finally speaks—or tries to.

The new hero has cut himself off from cultural and social life and now seems close to abdicating even from himself. Whether he throws words on a page, like the San Francisco novelist Jack Kerouac, or pigment onto a canvas like the "action" painter Franz Kline, whether he mumbles through a movie or shimmies in the frenetic gyrations of rock-'n-roll, he is a man belligerently exalting his own inarticulateness. He "howls" when he has the energy, and when he doesn't, sits around "beat" and detached, in a funk. He is hostile to the mind, petulant toward tradition, and indifferent to order and coherence. He is concerned chiefly with indulging his own feelings, glorifying his own impulses, securing his own "cool" kicks. His most characteristic sound is a stammer or a saxophone wail; his most characteristic symbol, a blotch and a glob of paint.

He exults in solitude and frequently speaks proudly of his "personal vision." Yet, while outwardly individualistic and antisocial, he is inwardly conformist. He travels in packs, writes collective manifestoes, establishes group heroes like the late movie star James Dean, and adheres to the ethics of the coterie. He is "existential" without having developed any substantial existence. If he has a coherent philosophy, it is one of simple negation without any purposeful individual rebellion to sustain it.

The novelists and poets now centering in San Francisco are the most striking examples of conformists masquerading as rebels. They travel together, drink together, "smoke pot"

Customers at a North Beach bar in San Francisco's Bohemia observe Sunday by listening to a tape recording of Allen Ginsberg's "Howl." Jazz often provides background for Beat Generation poetry readings.

JACK KEROUAC

Start of his novel *The Subterraneans:*

Once I was young and had so much more orientation and could talk with nervous intelligence about everything and with clarity and without as much literary preambling as this; in other words this is the story of an unself-confident man, at the same time of an egomaniac, naturally, facetious won't do—just to start at the beginning and let the truth seep out, that's what I'll do—. It began on a warm summernight—ah, she was sitting on a fender with Julien Alexander who is . . . let me begin with the history of the subterraneans of San Francisco . . .

Julien Alexander is the angel of the subterraneans, the subterraneans is a name invented by Adam Moorad who is a poet and friend of mine who said "They are hip without being slick, they are intelligent without being corny, they are intellectual as hell and know all about Pound without being pretentious or talking too much about it, they are very quiet, they are very Christlike." Julien certainly is Christlike. I was coming down the street with Larry O'Hara old drinking buddy of mine from all the times in San Francisco in my long and nervous and mad careers I've gotten drunk and in fact cadged drinks off friends with such "genial" regularity nobody really cared to notice or announce that I am developing or was developing, in my youth, such bad freeloading habits though of course they did notice but liked me and as Sam said "Everybody comes to you for your gasoline boy, that's some filling station you got there" or say words to that effect—old Larry O'Hara always nice to me, a crazy Irish young businessman of San Francisco with Balzacian backroom in his bookstore where they'd smoke tea and talk of the old days of the great Basie band or the days of the great Chu Berry—of whom more anon since she got involved with him too as she had to get involved with everyone because of knowing me who am nervous and many leveled and not in the least one-souled—not a piece of my pain has showed yet—or suffering—Angels, bear with me—I'm not even looking at the page but straight ahead into the sadglint of my wallroom and at a Sarah Vaughan Gerry Mulligan Radio KROW show on the desk in the form of a radio . . .

(PUBLISHED BY GROVE PRESS, INC.)

together, publish together, dedicate works to each other, share the same pony-tailed girls in faded blue jeans, wear a uniform costume, and take for their collective theme the trials and tribulations of their own troubled souls. "I saw the best minds of my generation destroyed by madness, starving hysterical naked," writes Allen Ginsberg, the most talented of the group, before launching into a description of the worst degradations to which the human animal can descend. The only horror not included in it is loneliness, for the Beat Generation suffers its degradations en masse.

Although they pretend to "disaffiliate" from the "Social Lie," Ginsberg, Kerouac, William Burroughs, Michael McClure, Michael Rumaker and other writers of the Generation are the Joiners of the new age, eschewing the Lions and the Shriners for a club whose rules, though more unusual, are no less strict. Their extremely limited language, derived from the "hip" talk of "cool" jazz musicians, is a coterie argot designed to exclude the common run of "squares" who don't "dig" their message. But the coterie's message has an automatism about it that exposes its communal roots. Only Ginsberg ever expresses anger, the emotion of rebellion. The rest are either "cool," detached, separated from the world and their own existences, or brimming full of an indiscriminate enthusiasm for everything.

Take Jack Kerouac. His novel *On The Road* (1957), is a picaresque work in which the author, under a pseudonym, speeds from place to place across the country, usually in a car at up to 110 miles per hour, embracing people, cities, plains, and mountains. The book has an unflagging Whitmanesque zing and demonstrates that Kerouac, like most Americans, worships pure physical energy:

The only people for me are the mad ones, the ones who are mad to live, mad to talk, mad to be saved, desirous of everything at the same time, the ones who never yawn or say a commonplace thing, but burn, burn, burn like fabulous yellow roman candles exploding like spiders across the stars and in the middle you see the blue centerlight pop and everybody goes "Awww!"

Kerouac's most typical response is "Wow," but he makes sure to keep his feelings uncommitted and his energy undirected. In fact, he embraces everything on equal terms: "We love everything . . . we dig it all. We're in the vanguard of a new religion." And Kenneth Rexroth, a poet from another generation who is trying to give his own meaning to the movement, like an elder politician running on a young man's ticket, sees in this and other expressions like it a new affirmation of faith, reflecting a "reverence for life."

It is clear, however, that Kerouac's "reverence for life," like that of his friends, is actually a disguised disgust and boredom with life. For to be "desirous of everything at the same time" is really to be happy with nothing. It is no accident that Kerouac's characters are constantly seeking new kicks outside the pale of everyday experience: the experience of everyday life never touches them. In that speeding car, only the objects move (as if seen in a rearview projector giving the illusion of movement behind stationary actors) while the characters stand immobile. Never learning or growing or developing, they remain perpetually hungry until the inevitable disenchantment sets in:

[I wished] I were a Negro, feeling that the best the white world offered was not enough ecstasy for me, not enough life, joy, kicks, darkness, music, not enough night . . . I wished I were a Denver Mexican, or even a poor overworked Jap, anything but what I was so drearily, a "white man" disillusioned.

This attempt to identify one's self with dispossessed minorities is the hipster's effort to adopt a ready-made motivation for his rebellion. In its discontent with physical limitations, it also reflects an effort to escape from the self. This escape takes other forms in "dreams . . . drugs . . . waking nightmares, alcohol . . ." as poet Ginsberg, who celebrates the more sinister side of the movement, puts it. Under these influences, hallucinations are hailed as visions. Ginsberg's "angelheaded hipster" seeks "the ancient heavenly connection to the starry dynamo in the machinery of night," and if he can't find it with the aid of the various narcotics he mentions, he turns to "Plotinus Poe St. John of the Cross telepathy and bop kaballa," not to mention Zen Buddhism. For the hipster, these philosophies are designed to initiate him not into life but into nothingness. Thus:

For just a moment I had reached the point of ecstasy that I had always wanted to reach, which was the complete step across chronological time into timeless shadows, and wonderment at the bleakness of the mortal realm, and the sensation of death kicking at my heel to move on . . .

Here Kerouac is explicitly celebrating the attractiveness of death, just as Ginsberg frequently writes of his desire to curl up in the soft comfort of the womb. The other side of complete acceptance, then, is complete rejection, withdrawal into the "cool" neutral realm of perfect passivity. The opposite of "mad" is "beat"—and Kerouac defines "beat" as "beatific." One might more accurately, in describing this movement, talk of its reverence for death, since it leads its advocates into the bottomless void.

Although it embodies a vague intellectuality, this literary movement is persistently anti-intellectual. "I DON'T KNOW I DON'T CARE AND IT DOESN'T MAKE ANY DIFFERENCE," Kerouac affirms in his "philosophical final statement," and the stammering hero of his second book, *The Subterraneans*, bears him out: "Details are the life of it," he shouts; "say everything on your mind, don't hold it back, don't analyze or anything as you go along." Before this indiscriminate accumulation of details—the hallmark of the new writing— order, analysis, form, and eventually coherence give way. The result is a style like automatic writing or an Eisenhower press conference, stupefying in its unreadability. Most of

HARRY REDL

ALLEN GINSBERG

Opening lines of his poem "Howl":

I saw the best minds of my generation destroyed by madness, starving hysterical naked,

dragging themselves through the negro streets at dawn looking for an angry fix,

angelheaded hipsters burning for the ancient heavenly connection to the starry dynamo in the machinery of night,

who poverty and tatters and hollow-eyed and high sat up smoking in the supernatural darkness of cold-water flats floating across the tops of cities contemplating jazz,

who bared their brains to Heaven under the El and saw Mohammedan angels staggering on tenement roofs illuminated,

who passed through universities with radiant cool eyes hallucinating Arkansas and Blake-light tragedy among the scholars of war,

who were expelled from the academies for crazy & publishing obscene odes on the windows of the skull,

who cowered in unshaven rooms in underwear, burning their money in wastebaskets and listening to the Terror through the wall,

who got busted in their public beards returning through Laredo with a belt of marijuana for New York,

who ate fire in paint hotels or drank turpentine in Paradise Alley, death, or purgatoried their torsos night after night

with dreams, with drugs, with waking nightmares . . .

who chained themselves to subways for the endless ride from Battery to holy Bronx on benzedrine until the noise of wheels and children brought them down shuddering mouth-wracked and battered bleak of brain all drained of brilliance in the drear light of Zoo,

who sank all night in submarine light of Bickford's floated out and sat through the stale beer afternoon in desolate Fugazzi's, listening to the crack of doom on the hydrogen jukebox . . .

(PUBLISHED IN *Evergreen Review*, VOL. 1, NO. 2, BY GROVE PRESS, INC.)

The late James Dean became a teen-age idol through his projection of inarticulate youth in Rebel Without a Cause. *Typically, the hero is submissive only with his girl friend.*

the San Franciscans' works are like the modern "cool" jazz that forms the background against which they are often read aloud: the main theme founders and breaks down under a welter of subjective variations. Kerouac, Ginsberg, McClure, and the others fling words on a page not as an act of communication but as an act of aggression; we are prepared for violence on every page.

Although the San Franciscans talk a great deal about "essences," the only feeling one gets from their work about the essence of life is that it is upsettingly discontinuous and jerky and that it alternates between aggression and passivity. It is no accident that many of them are followers of the late Wilhelm Reich, a maverick psychiatrist who treated patients by placing them in the "orgone box" he had invented. His box might well be the monument to their movement: for in it, cultural withdrawal is complete, will and intelligence are suspended, and the emotions are at the mercy of mysterious "cosmic" stimuli.

The mixed aggression and passivity of the hipster literati are an index of the adolescent quality of their rebellion. So is their accent on youth; about the only crime offensive to all of them is that of growing old. Juvenile delinquency, on the other hand, is often a subject for glorification, since it is an expression of spontaneous feelings. Dean Moriarity, one of the central characters of *On The Road* (and also the secret hero of Ginsberg's poem, "Howl"), is too confused to speak clearly, but he expresses himself by stealing cars, taking drugs, and conning his friends. Moriarity's childish irresponsibility has in it something so poignant that Kerouac hails him as a "new kind of American saint." Other subjects for canonization by the San Franciscans are the motor-

cycle set—Ginsberg's "saintly motorcyclists" and Kerouac's "Texas poets of the night"—whose angelic deeds are daily immortalized in quite a different way on the country's police blotters. It is hardly a coincidence that the argot of teen-age gangs and of the hipster literati is almost identical. It is not so long a jump from the kick-seeking poet to the kick-seeking adolescent who, sinking his knife into the flesh of his victim, thanked him for the "experience."

It is significant that the heroes and saints of the Beat Generation are all death lovers and escapists. The junkies, the derelicts, the delinquents, the madmen, the criminals, and the Outsiders who people this literature have in common their paralysis in the face of all intelligible forms of behavior. In this they are counterparts of the personification created on the level of popular culture by Marlon Brando and aped by large numbers of Stanislavsky Method actors since. In *The Wild One*, for example, Brando played a "saintly motorcyclist," equipped with leather jacket, studded belt, and violent nature, of the type Ginsberg and Kerouac exalt in their writing. Brando, who has a strong social conscience, has expressed regret at his participation in this film and lately has even been attempting roles of a more articulate nature. But the success of his imitators— James Dean, Ralph Meeker, Ben Gazzara, Paul Newman, Rod Steiger, and countless others—testifies to the persistent popularity of a hero unlike any before seen in the movies.

Like the heroes of San Francisco literature, this hero is extremely withdrawn, but his subjectivity seems as much the result of the actor's technique as of the scenarist's concept. The famous Method of the Russian director Stanislavsky, as presently practiced in this country, exalts the actor's personality over the written word. That is, the actor imposes his experience on the part rather than—like, say, Sir Laurence Olivier—subordinates himself to it. The personality of many Method actors, however, rather than being an individual expression, is often a parody of Brando's playing of Stanley Kowalski. The result of this imitation is a culture hero with easily distinguishable traits. Important among them is that he is usually a delinquent of some kind and that—for all the dependence of his media on language —he cannot talk.

The hero's link with the Beat Generation is signified by the fact that he is invariably an outcast or a rebel who stands in a very uneasy relationship with society. His rebellion, like that of the San Francisco writers, is expressed as much through his costume (torn T shirt, leather jacket, blue jeans) as through his behavior, for in a world of suits and ties, a shabby, careless appearance is an open sign of alienation. Again as in the case of the San Franciscans, his rebellion seems to be unmotivated. It no longer has any political or social relevance, and it is obscured by his inability to describe it. Most often, he is a rebel without a cause, whose sense of grievance has turned inward on himself, making his grip on reality extremely uncertain. Although he often travels in groups, sometimes in juvenile gangs, he seems to be alienated even from his friends. He is a man whom nobody understands and who understands nobody. Toward the world of authority—his father, his teachers, and the police—he feels hostile and he seems to be submissive only with his girl friend. His confusion has isolated him within a self which he cannot comprehend and which, in consequence, causes him unspeakable pain.

In this character, the inarticulate hero appears in a number of movies that despite surface differences never seem to change in essential parts. More timorous than literature and subject to rigid production codes, these movies do not glorify the hero's delinquency (he is usually converted to righteousness before the end), but they do their best to exploit it. His violent nature, for example, is allowed expression but is channeled into the service of benevolence; it is directed always against the "bad guys" and helps the hero to move over to the right side.

In *On The Waterfront*, Marlon Brando is an ex-prize-fighter who works on the docks. He is isolated even from his peers and can find consolation only in homing pigeons. When his brother is murdered, he decides, despite his hatred of the police, to inform on the labor racketeers who killed him and, at the end, engages in a bloody fist fight with the thugs. In *Rebel Without a Cause*, the young hero (James Dean) cannot come to terms with his family or gain acceptance by his adolescent contemporaries. To win the friendship of the latter, he agrees to play "chicken" with hot-rod cars, a game which results in the death of the gang's leader. Unable to tell the police or his father, he is attacked by the revenging gang. In *Edge of the City*, a friendless wanderer (John Cassavetes) on the run from the police, gets a job as a longshoreman and is shown the ropes by a fatherly Negro. When the Negro is slain in a brutal hook fight, he battles with the vicious foreman who killed his friend.

Despite the fact that it is invariably represented as a benevolent social gesture, the hero's violence, along with his inarticulateness, exposes his antisocial nature. He rejects communication with the outside world and yields to his basic impulses. Whatever intelligence he has is subordinated to his feelings. But even the emotions of this hero are blunted and brutalized. It is significant that he rarely exhibits anger, the civilized expression of the aggressiveness he feels, but only violence, its primitive expression. He remains "cool" until the moment comes to strike. Without a language, he cannot understand or express his feelings; he can only act them out. Like Melville's Billy Budd, who could express himself only with a blow because of his stuttering speech, the movie hero illustrates his feelings most characteristically with his fists.

Early this year, a rock-'n-roll jamboree at Boston led to riots, and it is clear that the Beat Generation hero, like certain rock-'n-roll singers, reflects anarchic impulses in the young. Rejection of coherent speech for mumbles, grunts, and physical gyrations is a symptom of this anarchy, for speech is an instrument of control. Rebelliousness has always been essential to any awakening of the young, for it leads them to question existing values, to pierce lifeless conventions, and to erect a moral or a social structure more true to life as they see it. But today's rebellion can define neither its own values nor those of the authority it rejects. Such juvenile rebellion, rather than being a true expression of individualism, stems from an impulse to belong and usually ends in some kind of conformity. The memorial cult that developed after the death of James Dean had no program except "togetherness." Similarly, the one reward to which the hero of these movies aspires is acceptance by the group. His conflict has been caused not by considered intellectual disagreement but by misunderstanding—that is, he is thought to be hostile because he cannot express his true feelings. But although most of these films end with the hero's acceptance by society or by the gang or by his father (as in the case of Dean's characters), nothing has truly been resolved. The inarticulate hero never makes the lonely step to maturity. When James Dean grows to middle age in *Giant*, his character doesn't change; he merely has some powder added to his hair.

The difference between the new rebellion and the earlier one of the 1930's in the theater can be seen in their contrasting types of expression. Although the new hero descends from the older "social-protest" drama (he wears the same shabby costume as the proletarian hero of those days), some

Elvis Presley receives congratulations from RCA Victor's Steve Sholes on reaching his 16th million in record sales.

highly significant changes have been made. The actors and writers of the old Group Theater were highly articulate people, rather than stammerers. John Garfield, Luther Adler, and Lee J. Cobb, the most representative actors in the group, were notable for their direct delivery, the intensity of their emotions, and their poetic intelligence; and Clifford Odets was one of America's most dynamic and eloquent playwrights. Furthermore, Odets' characters were fully engaged in the world and highly aware of the forces against which they were rebelling. One could disagree with the playwright's interpretation of social events, but only because one always knew precisely what his meaning was. The new acting and writing, on the other hand, is remarkable for its de-emphasis of language and its brutalization of character. The inarticulate hero portrays no feeling at all directly. He is persistently engaged in playing *against* his emotions.

A scene from *On The Waterfront* illustrates the two approaches. Brando, playing a dockworker, comes into conflict with the veteran Lee J. Cobb, playing a labor boss. The two actors confront each other across a table, both presumably fighting mad. Cobb communicates this directly, manipulating his bulk, slamming on the table, thrusting out his jaw, letting his power erupt across the room. Brando, on the other hand, suppresses his emotions, examining his fingers, shifting in his chair, surveying his antagonist with an intense but blank expression, stammering quietly, simmering rather than boiling. Both are using the subjective Stanislavsky Method, but the technique leads Cobb to reveal himself, Brando to hide. Cobb's anger is kinetic, explosive, articulate, while Brando's is repressed, internalized, and "cool." Brando is "beat"; he never raises his voice, but we know that the character he plays will momentarily spring into violence. Cobb has contact with things and people; Brando is alone in his own private world.

While the present school of Abstract Expressionist and "action" painters in America may at first glance seem far removed from the Brandos and Jimmy Deans and Kerouacs, they too have moved into private worlds. Their manifestoes are defiant repudiations of the world beyond the self and of any art concerned with representing something external to it. The Abstract Expressionist's attitude toward his surroundings is illustrated by the new function he gives his work: his painting is no longer a gate opening onto a world of forms and ideas but a wall on which he inscribes his personal state of mind. The frenzied arabesques of Jackson Pollock, the calligraphic images of Franz Kline and Robert Motherwell, the huge horizontal blocks of Mark Rothko, the frosty specters of Clyfford Still, the "bursts" and "blasts" of Adolph Gottlieb, are all concerned not with things or with people but with the artist's responses to his own mystic visions. In these "action" paintings we are confronted with the painter's dreams before he has reflected on them, sometimes before he even knows what they are. "When the painting is finished," writes one of their number, "the subject reveals itself."

In short, the Abstract Expressionists do not seem hostile to reality around them so much as completely indifferent to it. As far as these painters are concerned, the outside world might just as well not exist. They seek in their own souls for mystical states which they can transfer to canvas as "flux," "nonrational truths," and "personal myths." The painter no longer feels a need to describe or to reflect upon his subject but rather, like Grace Hartigan, to "distill it until I have its essence." When we hear more talk about "essences," we are on familiar territory. The spilled ink, the spattered paint, and the dripped pigment are expressions of "spontaneity," much like Kerouac's automatic writing. Drawing almost disappears, while color, with its exclusively emotional attack, becomes predominant. The intelligence is suspended in favor of intuitions, feelings, impulses.

One is hard put to test the validity of these feelings and impulses, since no one seems to know quite what they are. The latest abstract paintings deal with an "unknown realm of experience" and are therefore designed to suggest emotions unaccountable to reason. Since these emotions are nonrational, it becomes impossible to discourse about them. The painter Clyfford Still finds "demands for communication . . . both presumptuous and irrelevant." The painting is not to be explained or understood but rather *experienced*. Since the painting is now a feeling rather than an object, it can only call forth a subjective response. In fact, the spectator is expected to have a response to a response, ideally the same response as the artist. He is no longer to see through the painter's eyes but simply to vibrate in tune with his unconscious mind.

The result is a pictorial parallel to the mumbling Method performance and the stammering San Francisco novel —an exercise in noncommunication, which forces one to take the artist's "higher vision" on faith alone. The paintings no doubt have a certain validity, but validity of a very limited and relative kind, like a Rorschach test which conjures up different associations in each spectator. The Abstract Expressionist's reluctance to communicate concretely casts serious doubts on his insights. An artist is under no compulsion to communicate, but it is nonsense to assume that he is more profound if he cannot get through with his feelings and ideas.

In fact, in this new art it is often difficult to distinguish between self-expression and self-indulgence. The feeling most powerfully reflected in Pollock's work is aggression,

CONTINUED ON PAGE 134

One of New York's younger Abstract Expressionists is Theodoros Stamos, who has exhibited ever since he was twenty and is represented in the Metropolitan, Whitney, Modern Art, San Francisco, Baltimore, and other museums. Behind him stands his In Memoriam II, *which according to the artist was found to have "unconscious symbols" in it.*

A CASE OF COEXISTENCE:

CHRISTENDOM AND THE TURKS

By H. R. TREVOR-ROPER

To us the great fact of the fifteenth and sixteenth centuries is the expansion of Europe by the spectacular discovery of new continents; to contemporaries it was its diminution by the spectacular advance of the Turkish Empire. In France, between 1480 and 1609, twice as many books were published on the Turks as on America, and the greatest of the observers of Turkey, the Belgian Busbecq, complained that the nations of Christendom were gathering worthless empires at the end of the world while losing the heart of Europe. Throughout the sixteenth century Europeans were alternately fascinated and terrified by the Turks—by their silent, invincible, victorious armies, by their mixture of cruelty and toleration, their system of political slavery, and their private moral virtues. Alternately the rulers of Europe preached crusades and practiced appeasement of this terrible enemy, whom only his eastern enemies—first Tamerlane, then the Sophy of Persia—seemed to restrain from swallowing up their whole continent.

"When the Turks have settled with Persia," wrote Busbecq, "they will fly at our throats, supported by the might of the whole East; how unprepared we are, I dare not say. . . . Constantinople, once the rival of Rome, is now laid low in wretched slavery. Who can look on without pity, without reflecting on the mutability of human things? Besides who knows whether the same fate may not now be threatening our own land?"

For already, when he wrote, the bastions of Eastern Europe had crumbled: Belgrade had fallen by land and Rhodes by sea; the Turkish armies had conquered the plains of Hungary and their fleets dominated the Western Mediterranean from Algiers.

The Europeans had reason to be fascinated by the Turks, for these new conquerors were unlike any others they had known. They were not a nation; they were a host of peoples, an imperial family, and a system. The sultan's subjects were of diverse conquered races, his invincible janissaries had all been born Christians, his terrible sea captains were almost invariably renegades; his technicians, his financiers, his merchants were Christians or Jews. What power had made these men desert their natural traditions and uphold a slave empire so utterly at variance with European society?

European society was an aristocratic and landed society, a society of hierarchy, heredity, and privilege; the Ottoman Empire knew no aristocracy, no class loyalties, no heredi-

tary privilege outside the sultan's own family, whose privilege was limited to the alternative of the throne or the bowstring. Wherever the Turks imposed direct rule, the old aristocracies were liquidated and a new social system was implanted on their ruin. In Budapest Busbecq saw the splendid palaces of the Hungarian nobles, recently so powerful, all in ruins; in Bulgaria he found descendants of the royal house married to plowmen and shepherds; in Constantinople he saw members of the imperial families of Palaeologus and Cantacuzene reduced to menial trades. These were the few who had survived the general massacres of the nobility, and Busbecq was one of the few who could see them; for in general the Turks, having conquered a country and imposed their social system, protected it by an iron curtain from profane eyes. On crossing the frontier from Vienna to Budapest he felt as if he were entering another world, so different was it from the old Europe of which so lately it had been a part.

A hideous system, Europeans thought; and yet, since it had been accepted willingly by so many of their former subjects, they were obliged to concede its merits, or their defects. Why, they asked, had it so triumphed? The answer stared them in the face. Europe, in the days of Turkish conquest, had not only been politically divided, it had been full of social unrest. The aristocratic system in Eastern Europe had become intolerable. Landlordism on the Continent, colonialism and monoculture in the islands, had everywhere bred a mutinous native peasantry ready to welcome the Turk as a deliverer from social bondage. The Hungarian chivalry that went down fighting in the valley of the Danube and the Venetian galleys that watched the loss of Greece and its islands were the forces of an alien oligarchy whose subjects preferred—or thought they preferred—the Turks. Constantinople itself—a medieval Shanghai controlled by Venetian and Genoese concessionaires—hardly resisted its change of masters. Three years after its fall, a German popular play, the *Türkenspiel*, represented the sultan coming to Nuremberg as the Messiah of the poor peasants. Eighty-five years later Luther, whose great hymn *Eine feste Burg* may well have been written to inspire an imperial crusade against the Turks, nevertheless declared that the German peasantry, crushed by noble landlords, might well prefer Turkish rule to that of such Christian lords.

Thus, for some two centuries, from the disastrous crusade of Nicopolis in 1396 to the peace of 1606, the aristocratic society of Western Europe, like the liberal society of Western Europe today, looked with apprehension on the portentous new power in the East: a power of huge military strength, which, exploiting every social discontent, had advanced into the heart of Europe, imposed a new social system, and protected it behind an iron curtain; a power, moreover, that by its very success fascinated many of those who sought to resist it. Half the contemporary books on Turkey are inspired by admiration as well as by fear and hatred. Even the imperial ambassador could not withhold his respect from the civic virtue, the charitableness, the frugality, the public works, and the *carrière ouverte aux talents* that he found in the Ottoman Empire, and grudgingly admitted that slavery, after all, has its social utility. From overpopulated Southern Europe there was a constant stream of emigration to those hospitable lands of opportunity where, it was noted, there were no beggars; and persecuted intellectuals—Jews of Spain and Germany, Protestants of Italy—fled, or dreamed of fleeing, to that tolerant empire where religion at least was free. To the rulers of Western Europe all this was an added source of alarm. What were they to do? The answer was given by their traditional oracle, the Pope of Rome: Christians unite! Prepare for a crusade against the ideological enemy, the conquering tyrant!

And what did they do in fact? They quarreled among themselves, split Christendom in two, mopped up empires overseas, and while all vying with each other in denouncing the infamous Turk, each secretly made, or sought to make, alliances with him against the others. The king of France, by his alliance, obtained profitable concessions for his subjects and, in return, welcomed a Turkish army in France. In *Europe and the Turk*, Dorothy Vaughan writes: "Christian captives were openly sold in Toulon market-place, and while French Protestants were undergoing savage persecution, Turks on French soil turned unmolested to Mecca to pray." The king of Spain taxed his subjects regularly for the crusade and as regularly pocketed the proceeds. Venice for the sake of old markets, England for new, managed and supplied the infidel. Lutheran Germany, suspicious of all papal crusades, insisted that "to reform our ways and works is the best defence against the Turks."

The Jesuits, having once got a footing in Constantinople for the purpose of missionary work, quickly changed their tune and concentrated on the more congenial task of denouncing Protestant and Greek Christians to the common enemy. As for the Pope himself, when it came to the point he always found himself too poor for any action —perhaps even (like Alexander VI) he was in receipt of a Turkish pension. . . . It was all very unedifying and ought, of course, as Busbecq foresaw, to have led to a Turkish con-quest of Europe. In fact it did not. Whereas a crusade might have proved as disastrous as the crusade of Nicopolis, this refusal of a crusade led to a long practical coexistence, until suddenly, in the seventeenth century, it became clear that the danger was past. Europe, in full internecine vigor, then observed the decay of the Turkish empire, and having failed to unite against the tyrant in his prime, soon had to unite to prop him up when he had become "the sick man of Europe."

How had it happened? The rise and fall of nations remains a historical mystery which cannot be solved in a paragraph. We know very little of Turkish history, and what we know is almost entirely drawn from the imperfect observation of foreigners; for the Turks themselves have, until recently, been incurious in such matters. As Busbecq wrote, "they have no idea of chronology and dates and make a wonderful mixture and confusion of all the epochs of history." Probably the breakdown was institutional: the collapse of that system of privileged slavery which, under able sultans, had given a formidable but temporary cohesion to an otherwise ramshackle empire. Perhaps it was also economic: the Turkish, like the Roman and the Spanish empires, created no new wealth—it lived parasitically on foreign wealth and faltered when that supply ran out. Possibly a complex "liberal" society has, after all, greater staying power—because it has greater resilience—than a "classless" tyranny. We cannot say. But even so, even if we must leave this deep question open, at least there is one negative conclusion that we can draw from this historical precedent: The theory that the world cannot live "half slave and half free," that a frontal struggle between opposing systems is sooner or later inevitable and might as well be hastened by an ideological crusade, is simply not true. Europe and the Turk, with their opposing ideologies and opposing social systems, faced each other for centuries. There were diplomatic relations and local struggles, as between Christian powers, but there was no crusade; and when the system that had once seemed so formidable began to disintegrate, it was through inner weakness.

Today these facts are worth remembering. Our Marxist historians like to compare the opposition between Bolshevism and the West with the struggle between barbarian Christianity and the decadent pagan empire of Rome. They do so because they know that the barbarians prevailed.

All historical parallels are imperfect and therefore dangerous; but those who use them would do well to remember one which, being inconvenient, they too often forget: the parallel of coexistence, of Europe and the Turk.

H. R. Trevor-Roper is Regius Professor of Modern History at Christ Church, Oxford. The foregoing essay appears in his new book of historical studies, Men and Events, *published by Harper & Brothers.*

Suleiman the Magnificent

47

MONDADORI PRESS

Nowhere on earth, perhaps, are the land and the people in happier balance than in Bali. The rich green rice valleys and the terraced hills are cultivated like a garden by the Balinese, some of whom are here climbing a hill bearing gifts to their gods. These gods forbid any disturbance of the natural order.

It is Sir Julian Huxley's contention that, if the earth is to nourish its growing billions, in body and spirit, man must plan and preserve a harmonious relationship with nature. For the first time in history he has the power—and the urgent necessity—to develop the planet to meet the needs of the human race.

MAN'S CHALLENGE:

THE USE

OF THE EARTH

THE WORLD POPULATION EXPLOSION

DEMANDS THAT MAN PLAN THE

FUTURE OF HIS TERRESTRIAL HOME

By JULIAN HUXLEY

People often maintain that the discovery of how to release atomic energy has brought us to the brink of a new epoch, equivalent in importance to the beginning of the industrial epoch two centuries ago, and overshadowing every other modern human development. However, I am a biologist, and actually am quite certain that it is in the field of human biology, and in particular of human numbers, that man is facing his greatest challenge. Owing to the advances of medical science and sanitation, a wholly new situation has arisen, which we may call "death control." The expectation of life at birth, which at the height of classical Roman civilization was only about 30 years, is now around 70 in technologically advanced Western nations. Mortality, especially infant mortality, is falling everywhere. As a result, a novel type of population increase has begun, a quite new spurt in human numbers has been initiated.

This is the first moment in human history when man has consciously faced the problem of his role in the evolution of this planet. Evolution operates by the successive rise of a series of dominant types. The last three have been reptiles, which were dominant during the Mesozoic epoch, from nearly 200 million to about 60 million years ago; the placental mammals, which were dominant during the Cenozoic, from about 60 million years ago; and finally, the human type, which began to show its potentialities during the ice age but did not become truly and fully dominant until postglacial times and the invention of agriculture. Do not let us forget how young man is, biologically speaking. His dominant phase has so far lasted less than 10,000 years, as against the scores of millions of years of earlier types. And he is still in the full tide of evolutionary change, though of course the method of his evolution is psychosocial, not biological—that is, by the transmission of tradition rather than by that of altered genes.

VENICE, 1958

She looks a sea Cybele, fresh from ocean,
Rising with her tiara of proud towers
At airy distance, with majestic motion,
A ruler of the waters and their powers . . .
The pleasant place of all festivity,
The revel of the earth, the masque of Italy.

So wrote Byron of Venice.
This was before the Coca Cola barge began to ply the Grand Canal.

At the dawn of civilization, say 5,000 years ago, the total population of the world cannot have numbered much more than 20 million. Today the mere yearly increase in world population is nearly twice this amount. Apart from occasional temporary setbacks, world population has steadily increased. It reached the billion mark in the 1850's and the two-billion mark in the 1920's.

Population is, of course, self-multiplying, like money at compound interest; and what is even more alarming than its absolute growth is that its compound interest rate of increase has also been steadily increasing. Before the discovery of agriculture the rate cannot have exceeded one-tenth of 1 per cent; 300 years ago it was less than half of 1 per cent, and it only reached 1 per cent well on in the present century. It is now about $1\frac{1}{3}$ per cent and is still increasing. Even with the aid of the industrial and technological revolution, whose beginnings we can date around 1650, it took nearly two centuries from that date to double world population; but unless some cataclysm occurs, today's population will double itself in less than fifty years from now. (One projection made by the United Nations Popula-

tion Branch envisages an even faster increase and estimates that by the year 2000, world population may exceed $6\frac{1}{4}$ billion.)

As a result, some of the more thoughtful men and women alive today are beginning to ask new questions about humanity. They are trying to consider the present situation of the world *sub specie evolutionis*. From the point of view of the continuing process of evolution, what are the functions for which the surface of our planet is needed, and how satisfactorily are they now being carried out? When we begin thinking along such lines, we find ourselves coming up against many facts, principles, and ideas which earlier generations did not bother their heads about.

There is first the obvious fact that the surface of the globe is limited. Man cannot envisage an indefinite increase in numbers (or in any human activity) but must begin thinking in terms of equilibria; the immensely rapid changes of the last few thousand years are symptoms of human youth and, indeed, immaturity. Whether we succeed in manufacturing synthetic nutriment or not, it is safe to prophesy that a large proportion of man's food will continue to be grown naturally, under cultivation, as it is today. In countries at a high technological level and with a high density of population, like Britain, there is already serious competition between the use of land for food production and for purposes such as housing, roads, and airfields. It is worth remembering that the area of London just about doubled between 1900 and 1950.

The absolute growth in size of cities is another result of general population growth. Cities like New York, Tokyo, or London have now reached a size at which they are defeating their own aims. Large numbers of their inhabitants have to spend two or three hours every day in great discomfort getting to and from their work, and the problems of traffic and parking seem to be approaching insolubility.

Besides food production, there is the problem of moisture conservation and the prevention of erosion. Large areas once covered by forest—for instance in China and in the Middle East—have been denuded of trees, the climate has been altered, and the fertile topsoil has been partly or wholly eroded away. A scientific survey could establish what area of the world's surface requires to be reafforested or otherwise devoted to antierosion measures.

But before pursuing the subject from the positive point of view, of the optimum use that man might make of his terrestrial home, let us look at it from the gloomiest possible angle. Hamlet apostrophized man as "the paragon of animals," and this is a fair description of our species as the latest dominant type in evolution—so long as he does not overreach himself. But if he allows himself to multiply unchecked, he is in danger of becoming the planet's cancer.

After all, what is a cancer? It is a monstrous, or pathological, growth whose cells have ceased to be controlled in their proliferation, have embarked on a course of unlimited multiplication, and have lost some or all of their organization. The cancer becomes a parasite on the organized body; its cells start invading and destroying normal tissues, and groups of them may get carried off in the blood stream to form the destructive secondary growths called metastases. Eventually the normal healthy body is killed by the cancer—either starved to death, or its healthy tissues eaten away or simply crowded out by the abnormal, overactive cancerous tissues.

Our planet is not an organism, but it is an organic system with interrelated parts. Water, soil, mineral resources, air, green plants and animals, bacteria and men—up until recently they have been held together in a web of balanced interdependence; and the whole system has evolved, slowly and majestically, through a series of self-transformations which have realized new and marvelous possibilities for the whole, especially for animal life. Until recently there has never been overmultiplication or overexploitation, by man any more than by any other organism. Human increase has been subjected to various checks and limitations—partly the same checks of disease and starvation and ruthless competition that apply to other animals, but also partly self-generated checks like war, or self-imposed limitations like infanticide or abstention from sexual intercourse.

But now unchecked multiplication is bringing about a state of affairs that can properly be called cancerous. Deforestation and bad methods of cultivation have caused aridity and erosion and have removed much of the soil that is the basis of food production. In the last century, man has started to live increasingly on capital resources—of coal, oil, and other minerals; he is using up in a few generations or centuries what it took tens of millions of years to accumulate. His per capita consumption of resources has steadily mounted, sometimes to a fantastic extent. Thus the consumption of metals and mineral fuels by the United States since 1918 exceeds the total consumed by the whole of mankind in all preceding history. No other species has ever shown this unbridled increase both in proliferation and in consumption. Nor did man himself during his early history.

And as the balance between resources and human numbers is upset, the quality of the population will, without question, go down. The earth will be bled white, all to maintain an excess of frustrated, underdeveloped, and essentially parasitic creatures. The conversion of the lord of creation into a cancer of earth will, it can be calculated, happen within a century unless something is done to prevent it. In biological evolution, successful animal types eventually become stabilized through automatic checks and balances. Modern man has emancipated himself from these; he needs to aim consciously at stabilization with the aid of deliberate checks and balances. We have reached a phase where the only alternative to man's becoming a pathological phenomenon is to practice a conscious population policy.

KEITH MARTIN

WALDEN POND, 1957

"Nothing so fair, so pure . . ." wrote Thoreau in Walden, *"lies on the surface of the earth. Sky water. It needs no fence. Nations come and go without defiling it." This is what happened at Walden last year, when, in the name of progress, a section of shore was cleared to set up a children's water safety program. In this instance the Thoreau Society got a restraining order to stop the bulldozers in their tracks.*

The spectacular spread of death control has made necessary a world-wide diffusion of birth control.

This brings me back to the positive aspect of the problem. As I suggested earlier, we have to get down to first principles and ask ourselves, What are the functions for which the surface of our planet is needed? What are those which its human population can most desirably perform? How can they best be carried out? If we like to put the question in a still more general way, What should be the aim of man? How should he, as the dominant organic type on earth, direct the future evolution of himself and his planet?

The most general answer is that he should aim at the maximum realization of possibilities. The mere quantitative increase in number of human beings is not itself a desirable aim: improvement of life and health, and quality and variety of experience and activity must be our goal.

One function of the earth whose importance we have only just begun to recognize is that of *wilderness*, the function of allowing men and women to get away from the complications of industrial civilization and make contact with fine scenery and unspoilt nature. Of course, it is not everyone

The human need for privacy finds a desperate solution on a Santa Monica beach.

who likes wilderness; perhaps luckily, a considerable number of people enjoy crowds and prefer their vacations to be organized. But wilderness-lovers constitute a sizable minority—and also include a sizable proportion of interesting characters and original thinkers. Wilderness is, in the long run, one of the major functions humanity demands from the surface of the globe. National parks and similar areas where the enjoyment of nature is paramount are attempts to meet this need. But, of course, wilderness is compatible only with a very low population density.

Then there is the function of scientific and natural conservation. Thus there must be areas in which the interests of wild life, or at least the interests of humanity in enjoying wild life, are paramount over those of agriculture, urbanization, or anything else. No one who has seen large animals in natural surroundings can forget the thrilling spectacle: it makes one realize the beauty and wonder, the interest and strangeness, of the achievements of evolving life. It has value in and for itself, and also for the conscious experiences which it can bring to us human beings. Vast quantities of big game and other large animals have been exterminated in the past hundred years—indeed, in the quarter-century since I saw swarms of wild antelopes and zebras and hippos, game has been wiped out over large areas of Africa—and

it is now clear that we must set aside areas in which their preservation, and not human cultivation or habitation, shall be paramount.

The same holds for smaller mammals, for birds both rare and common, for interesting and beautiful insects and plants. In addition to the enjoyment that wild creatures can provide, there is the scientific duty of preventing the extinction of species and of preserving at least samples of the world's various ecological habitats and communities. In the most general terms, the function of conserving nature is one to which we must assign a not inconsiderable area of the globe's surface.

Elsewhere, the function of watershed control and of preventing erosion will be paramount, and the job of growing trees will be the most important aim. In other words, over very considerable areas the production of forests, not of human beings or their food, will be the essential function. In various parts of the world, for instance in India, these two aims are already coming into conflict.

It is thus clear that we need a careful plan for the best exploitation of our planet's resources. Large sectors of its surface must never be allowed to develop a high population density; on them, other functions must prevail.

This would be so even if the human species were adequately nourished. Within the trifling time of three or four generations, unchecked human multiplication would bring human numbers and human density to a point of diminishing returns, after which the level of human fulfillment would start to go down instead of up. But the fact is far different. Actually about two-thirds of the more than 2½ billion people in the world today are inadequately nourished, either through sheer lack of calories or through lack of some vitamin or other dietary factor needed for full health, growth, and energy.

Thus what we need above all is an agreed world population policy, enabling us to reverse the present disastrous trend while at the same time remedying the plight of the malnourished majority. The present course is leading toward overexploitation of resources and overproduction of increasingly frustrated, overcrowded, and inadequately developed human specimens. So far, human history has been on the whole a record of progress; more human beings enjoying a higher degree of fulfillment have come into existence, and the upper level of human achievement has been progressively raised. But, as an evolutionist, I would definitely forecast that a doubling of present human numbers will mean a reversal of this progressive trend of human evolution. It will mean that the world's population will be overly dense, less well nourished and developed physically, and with reduced opportunities for enjoyment and fulfillment. Man will still be the biologically dominant type, but he will have embarked on a degenerative trend, a downward slope.

There is a gleam of hope on the horizon. Three powerful

countries—India, Japan, and China—now have official policies of population control, and official birth-control schemes have been set in train in a few dependent territories. The adoption of a population-control policy by China is of extreme importance, not only because China contains over 600 million people, but because it is a Communist country, and the Russian Communists have so far officially maintained a bitter ideological opposition to the whole notion. They have even gone so far as to assert that overpopulation is impossible because scientific and technical advance will always be adequate, and indeed to charge that the very idea of overpopulation is the invention of economists and sociologists who are the henchmen of Western capitalism and imperialism. The fact of the matter, of course, is that the U.S.S.R. is at the moment underpopulated; but it will be suffering from population pressure in a matter of three or four generations at the outside.

It is one of the most curious phenomena of the modern world that the Russian Communists and the Roman Catholics agree that birth control is wicked—about the only subject on which they are in agreement. We may hope that the Russians will be influenced by the policy of their powerful partner, China, as well as by the facts. And fortunately the Roman Catholic Church is not in principle opposed to all ideas of keeping down human numbers. On the occasion of the United Nations Conference on World Population in Rome, the Pope himself declared that excess population could be a very serious matter and lead to great distress, and he commended the study of the population problem to all thoughtful Catholics.

The goal now should be agreement on the part of the countries of the world on the need for a general policy of population control. It would obviously be best to have this supported by a large majority at the UN; but if this proved impossible, it would be much better than nothing to have adherence to such a policy proclaimed by even a group of nations—a new kind of NATO concerned with population instead of with defense.

Humanity needs to make up its mind as to the ultimate, or at least the dominant, purpose of human existence. Is it physical enjoyment in this world? Is it salvation in a world after death? Is it national power? Is it obedience to some superindividual code of morality? Is it knowledge? Is it wealth?

Personally, I can see no escape from the conclusion that man's dominant aim must be to continue the billion-year dominant trend of evolution toward greater fulfillment and the realization of more and better possibilities. Man is now the sole agent by which the evolutionary process can continue that trend; but that is no reason why this should happen automatically—it would be just as possible for his future history to be degenerative as for it to be progressive. In any case, the only way in which he can make sure that he is moving in the right direction is by utilizing to the full two of his unique properties—his capacity for conscious planning on the basis of scientific survey and comprehension and deliberate accumulation of knowledge, and his capacity for operating on a world-wide scale.

Once such a point of view is adopted and it is recognized that the existence both of too few and of too many people will interfere with human fulfillment, the way is open for a rational world policy.

The assumption that anything which makes it possible to keep more human beings alive—like new sources of food from the sea, or the manufacture of synthetic food in the laboratory—must be good and right, is at once seen to be

Punch, BEN ROTH AGENCY

"I SUPPOSE IT'S PSYCHONEUROSIS, BUT I'VE GOT AN AWFUL FEELING OF SOMETHING NASTY CREEPING UP ON ME."

Punch *cartoons the relentless crawl of the housing developments over the English countryside. The scene could as well be Long Island or the San Fernando Valley. Spreading suburbia has enveloped the big cities, while "interurbia" has joined them together in chains of solid settlements like the continuous "ribbon city" which stretches along the eastern United States coast from Boston to Washington.*

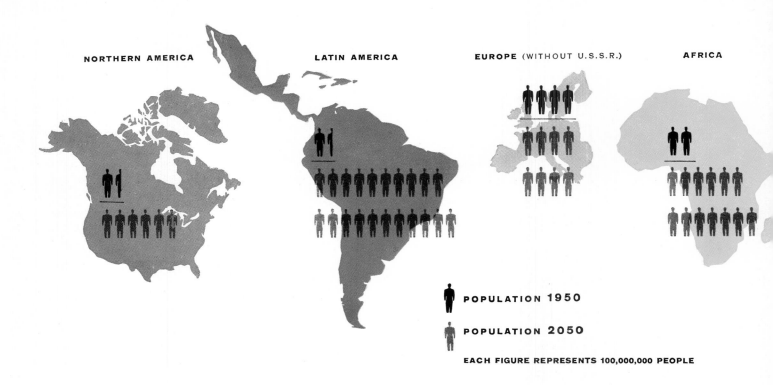

NORTHERN AMERICA   LATIN AMERICA   EUROPE (WITHOUT U.S.S.R.)   AFRICA

POPULATION 1950

POPULATION 2050

EACH FIGURE REPRESENTS 100,000,000 PEOPLE

fallacious. There must be an optimum magnitude for human numbers and human density. Below that general level, men will not have the opportunity to develop the sciences and the arts and their applications adequately, to produce noble architecture or efficient means of transport. Above that level, man will be, as it were, cutting off his nose to spite his face—he will be making life more inconvenient and less beautiful; will be making certain things, like the enjoyment of solitude and wild nature, impossible; will be destroying other living species; and will finally be condemning later generations to undernourishment, shortened life span, and general frustration.

One new symptomatic phenomenon of our epoch, brought about by the combination of increased human numbers and greater facility of transportation, has been the incipient vulgarization of the outstandingly beautiful cities created by man. To take one example, Venice is unique and is now becoming so overcrowded with tourists that enjoyment of its beauty is beginning to be interfered with. And we cannot very well produce duplicate Venices to meet the demand! The same sort of thing is beginning to happen to overly publicized places of natural beauty.

It is also worth remembering that once we manage to bring human quantity under some degree of control, we

The prospect of turning the Sahara into arable land, long a dream of engineers, has been enhanced by discovery of a high water table under much of the desert. This is an artificial oasis created by the French in Algeria. Wells have been sunk, date palms planted, and a wall of sand pushed up to protect the site from sandstorms. Another favorite scheme—digging a canal from the Mediterranean to irrigate the Sahara—depends on a cheap method of desalting sea water.

can make a beginning with the improvement of human quality—eugenics. And this would give our descendants an overriding aim for millennia to come; for the possibilities of fuller realization of health and energy, of intelligence and enjoyment, are virtually unlimited.

To sum up the problem, there are only two alternatives. One is to let population increase continue in the same

U.S.S.R.   **ASIA (WITHOUT U.S.S.R.)**   **OCEANIA**

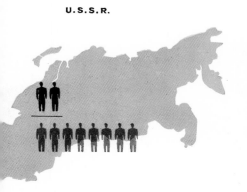
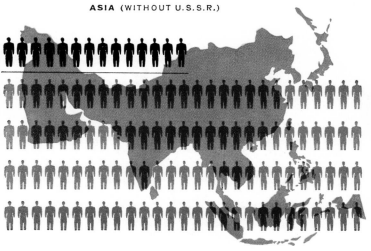

This chart presents one estimate of what the population of the world would be in the year 2050 if present rates of increase continue unchecked. The projection, based on statistics of the Population Branch of the United Nations, shows a total of 15,775,000,000, which markedly exceeds Sir Julian Huxley's estimate. Most experts, however, assume some decline in birth rates, especially in the Orient. A conservative prediction, made by Professor Harrison Brown of the California Institute of Technology, arrives at a total of 6,700,000,000 in 2050. The trends on which all predictions are based are, however, subject to alteration either by Malthusian checks of famine, war, and disease, or by deliberate control.

fashion as it has in the past. This will, without question, bring about a condition of world overpopulation and over-utilization of resources from which it will be hard to recover. The other alternative is to extend the method of science to human reproduction, and to study the entire problem thoroughly, with a view to a world population policy that shall be at one and the same time inspiring and practical.

BERNSEN'S INTERNATIONAL PRESS SERVICE, LTD., LONDON

As a preliminary, we need an authoritative study of what may be called "earth use," in which all the different factors involved in the future evolution of the earth as the home of man should be taken into account, from efficiency to beauty, from food production to speedy communication, from industrial development to the enjoyment of wild nature. A United Nations conference on the subject would be too cumbersome to ensure decisive results, though it might be useful in drawing the attention of governments to what is likely to be for most of them an unfamiliar subject; while small unofficial groups could not be expected to accomplish much beyond securing recognition of the importance of the idea. Perhaps the best solution would be for one of the great private foundations in the United States to set up such a project, calling on the best brains from many countries for their help.

The matter is urgent. The earth is already being badly misused today by its more than 2½ billion human inhabitants. Unless we do something about it, it will be worse misused by our grandchildren, who are pretty certain to number 5 billion. What is more, man is misusing himself by his unbridled multiplication. If we do nothing to prevent our grandchildren's grandchildren (less than a century and a half in the future) from numbering 10 or more billion, we shall deserve the obloquy of many generations to come.

Sir Julian Huxley, distinguished biologist and man of letters, is the author of a long list of books and scientific papers on subjects ranging from evolution and ethics to social planning and animal behavior. He was the first Director-General of the United Nations Educational, Scientific and Cultural Organization.

55

FROM
THE
SHAPELY
FORM
TO A
NEW ART
FORM

A revolution in the Broadway musical comedy since its Ziegfeld heyday has produced the new musical play with elements of drama, opera, and ballet

Future historians of the American theater may look on the last twenty years as lean ones in terms of new names, new ideas, or physical plant. While a few playwrights, producers, and stars have been born, many have died, dried up, or transplanted themselves to the dusty soil of Hollywood. Theaters that once glowed with the presence of a John Drew or Jeanne Eagels have been replaced by skyscrapers or permanently infiltrated by television quiz programs. Between the acts in those that remain, customers who have paid over eight dollars apiece for seats gaze on walls unpainted since the Harding Administration, stumble over threadbare lobby carpets, and hearken to the brays of vendors of orange drink.

Yet amid this partial desiccation there blooms an extraordinary flower. Musical comedy, once the theater's wayward girl—a creature of spangles, shrillness, and leers—has taken on surprising new vitality and form. Where once the musical was a localized kind of fun, designed solely for New Yorkers and visitors in town on a spree, it is today a new and refreshing art form—the only one of consequence to rise to the surface of the nation's cultural caldron in the last couple of decades.

Concurrently, the musical has cast off its local shackles. Today there are few metropolitan centers in the country that do not support at least one modern musical production, traveling or home-grown, during the course of a year. Most phenomenal of all is the sale of original-cast record albums of Broadway hits—including not just the ballads but plot songs, comedy songs, overtures, and interpolated ballet music as well—at around five dollars a copy. By an unusual inversion of Gresham's law, the good seems to be driving out the bad. The musicals which are best artistically (*Oklahoma!*, *My Fair Lady*, and others) also are most popular.

Here is a case in which the often-made claim that the taste of the American public is rising—a claim perhaps refutable in terms of automobiles, food, novels, and politicians—seems to be borne out. The musical has made such strides during the last fifteen years, in fact, that a number of cultural Cassandras are unable to agree on its next step, or even on whether there should be such a step.

Before considering this question, however, an analysis of this new art form is in order. We must begin by throwing out the descriptive term "musical comedy." Coined in the days of Weber & Fields to describe an entertainment cocktail composed in equal parts of gags, girls, and tunes, with a strong dash of improbability, it now correctly applies to only a few of the musicals that reach Broadway each season. Its place has now been assumed by what it is justifiable to call the "musical play"—a musical that possesses many of the characteristics of serious drama: a strong story line, a reasonably believable real-life setting, and characters with depth who change and develop as the plot progresses.

Like drama itself, the modern musical play has many different textures and colorings. It ranges all the way from the somber power of a *Porgy and Bess*, an almost operatic portrayal of primitive Negro life in the South, to the drugstore-cowboy jolliness of the *Pajama Game*, a breezy chronicle of slap-and-tickle in a midwestern sleepware factory. In all of its forms, however, the musical play employs dialogue, song, and dance in a continuous forward movement. Extraneous elements, however entertaining in themselves, are ruthlessly culled out in rehearsal or on the pre-Broadway road tour. The goal is a show so tight, so "integrated," that it holds its audience from start to finish in the grip of a single experience.

This is the goal of drama, as defined and expressed by no less an authority than Ibsen. When it is combined with the emotional power of superior music, the effect on an audience is often genuinely thrilling. This explains, in part, the great box office success of such outwardly disparate musical plays as *Carousel* and *Guys and Dolls*.

Broadway itself, from drama critics to ticket scalpers, has seized upon one word to characterize the musical play. That word, conveying high praise in the cliché-ridden lingo of show business, is *adult*. It expresses the theater's conviction that a mature art form of immense potentiality has reached the scene. It also stands as an inadvertent comment on the musical stage as it used to be.

Thirty years ago, for example, the theatergoer could choose between three well-defined types of musical show, all of which are now virtually extinct.

The operetta. Some of the most famous musicals ever produced in America fall into this category: *The Student Prince*, *Blossom Time*, *Naughty Marietta*, *Rose Marie*, *The New Moon*, *The Vagabond King*. Such shows specialized in piercing sopranos, virile tenors, and a great deal of lilting music generally written by Victor Herbert, Sigmund Romberg, or Rudolf Friml. Many songs from these shows are still heard; and although such lyrics as in "Indian Love Call" now seem insipid, the melodies have a power which still can excite an audience.

Yet operetta libretti had nowhere near the staying power

Bobby Clark   *Fanny Brice*   *Bert Lahr*   *W. C. Fields*   *Beatrice Lillie*   *Will Rogers*

of their music. They relied heavily on such old-chestnut devices as mistaken identity, forced (by the authors) misunderstandings or separations, and such gripping social problems as whether a criminal's sister could be happy with a Royal Canadian mountie. Short on humor, awash with sentimentality, musicals of this kind, once as popular as the Model T Ford and the novels of Gene Stratton Porter, now seem old-fashioned without being charming. The Great Depression, bringing with it a more down-to-earth outlook on life, banished the operetta from Broadway. After several successful farewell tours in the movies, conducted by Jeanette MacDonald and Nelson Eddy, the American operetta disappeared from the cultural scene.

The gag-and-girl show. There are two basic human desires which the theater is uniquely designed to satisfy. One is to laugh, which men and women enjoy equally. The other is to gaze on the female form, either uncostumed or superbly costumed, which men and women enjoy respectively. Musicals combining these two elements used to be standard fare of every Broadway season, with Florenz Ziegfeld the master chef. The Ziegfeld girls are legendary. The Ziegfeld stable of comedians included W. C. Fields, Will Rogers, Eddie Cantor, Leon Errol, Ed Wynn, and lesser lights. About twice a season, Ziegfeld used to put together either a Follies or a "book show" (meaning there was a plot of sorts) such as *Whoopee* or *Rio Rita*. One or two of the comedians would be engaged; a stable of writers and composers would be assigned to turn out a couple of hours' worth of material; lining up the girls was mostly a matter of a few phone calls.

To a contemporary audience, the "girls" part of the shows of Ziegfeld and his contemporaries would seem vulgar and overdone. The rise of the movies, advertising art, and sexually explicit literature has made the shapely show girl who did nothing but stand there in a thousand-dollar costume and a great big smile seem like pretty tame stuff. But many of the songs—"A Pretty Girl is Like a Melody," "Look for the Silver Lining," "I Can't Get Started With You"—are as pleasing today as when they were written.

What is perhaps most fondly remembered about these shows is how funny they were. The great comedians seen in them, after learning their trade in the rough-and-tumble worlds of burlesque and vaudeville, reached Broadway at the climax of their abilities: Will Rogers with his rope tricks and topical jokes; Fields with his famous twisted pool cue act; Cantor with his prancing feet, clapping hands, and slurred singing style; Fannie Brice in bloomers and a hair ribbon as Baby Snooks. In musical comedy these performers earned reputations and created characterizations that supported them in style for the rest of their working lives. This, in fact, is what really killed the gag-and-girl shows. The comedians were hired away from Broadway by Hollywood or radio, where most of them found they could make a great deal more money for working half as hard. Those who stayed behind—Bert Lahr, Jimmy Durante, Victor Moore, Bobby Clark—continued the gag show fitfully into the 1940's, when it finally succumbed.

There are many reasons why no signs of a revival have appeared, the chief one being that no new comedians have emerged who can touch the old-timers. Trained in a hard school, accustomed to theater audiences who could not be cued by "Applause" signs or rendered undiscriminating by night-club booze, the old-timers knew their trade inside out. They were protean performers. Most of them could sing, dance, juggle, play in blackface, tell jokes in dialect, and perform mild acrobatics. Each had a set of sketches, songs, characterizations, and comedy routines that had been tested before audiences from New Bedford to Butte and could be thrown in to bolster a sagging scene. Each was various enough in his accomplishments to carry a whole show almost alone.

In comparison, most of today's funny men seem pallid indeed. With no burlesque or vaudeville left in which to school themselves, all they can really do well is talk. This puts them at the mercy of writers and limits their effective appearance before an audience to the quarter hour taken up by the average night-club appearance or television "guest shot." Of them all, only two—Danny Kaye and Phil Silvers—have shown that they can carry a Broadway musical.

The topical show. "Satire is what closes Saturday night," is a dictum once enunciated by the playwright George S. Kaufman. Like many wisecracks, this one is more memor-

Three Elizas: Julie Andrews, Sally Ann Howes, Ann Rogers   *Three Higginses: Rex Harrison, Edward Mulhare, Brian Aherne*

able than true. Musical comedy, at least, had a long and successful tradition of satire. In the twenties and early thirties each Broadway season was highlighted by at least half a dozen successful revues or book shows devoted to poking fun—good humoredly or even savagely—at the passing scene. *The Garrick Gaieties* first brought to an appreciative public the chipper early songs of Rodgers and Hart:

> *We'll go to Yonkers*
> *Where true love conquers*
> *In the wilds;*
> *And starve together, dear*
> *In Childs'—*

The *Greenwich Village Follies*, the *Music Box Revues* (one of which launched the late Robert Benchley on his acting career in a monologue of his own composition, "The Treasurer's Report"), the *Little Shows*—such sassy, bright revues went through edition after edition, changing cast, songs, and book but holding their individual publics. On a grander scale, *The Band Wagon* stuck out its tongue at beer-drenched German *Gemütlichkeit* as Fred Astaire sang "I Love Louisa" in *Lederhosen;* a few minutes later his sister Adele and Frank Morgan found humor in the Depression and the self-pity that was so much a part of it by singing:

> *The outlook sure is gloomy,*
> *The landlord's about to sue me*
> *To get the rent that's long overdue—*
> *There's nothing quite as mean as*
> *Avoiding those subpoenas!*
> *I might as well be miserable with you.*

Book shows of the era also dealt with the life around them—at least superficially. *Good News* gave the low-down on coed colleges; *Follow Through* told all about the country club set; *Oh Kay* exposed bootleggers (and a girl named Kay who, in the person of Gertrude Lawrence, longed for "Someone to Watch Over Me"); in *Flying High* aviation marched onward from Lindbergh to Bert Lahr; *Of Thee I Sing*, most memorable of all, showed how to be elected President.

As the titles of these shows suggest, the humor they contained was often less than Shavian, and their plots sometimes left those who attended them with a slight feeling of

vertigo. *Red, Hot and Blue*, for example, dealt with the search for a missing sweetheart identifiable only through the scars left by a waffle iron she sat on at the age of four; but everything ended all right when Ethel Merman sang "It's Delovely."

The decline of these three types of show reflects changing American attitudes over the last four decades. Operetta faded away because it ceased to have much contemporary meaning during the volcanic changes of the post-1918 world. The gag-and-girl show perished because, in one way or another, its chief commodities—great comedians and sexual titillation—came to be widely available at less than Broadway prices. The topical show owes its decline to a factor that gives more cause for concern: Americans' seeming loss of ability to laugh at themselves.

World War II and the challenge of an atomically armed Communism have left in their wake a climate of uncertainty and tension that is discouraging to laughter. Unlike Europeans, we are not yet so accustomed to living under the gun that we can remain calm when reminded of our vulnerability. No matter how witty the reminder, our inclination is to skip the joke in favor of vilifying the jokester—or, at least, to defend what he pokes fun at.

Thus today, satire is out of fashion, in "poor taste," not generally enjoyed. In consequence it has largely vanished from all forms of public entertainment, including the musical stage. The wide popularity of the new musical play unquestionably stems in part from the fact that it is generally "serious" in theme and thus in emotional rapport with an unusually serious-minded public.

Although its era is widely considered to have begun with *Oklahoma!* (1943), the musical play did not suddenly develop in response to changes in public taste brought on by war. *Show Boat*, in 1927, foreshadowed much of what was to come. During the thirties, as the traditional elements of sentimentality, sex, and satire slowly disappeared from the musical theater, scattered elements of the developing form began to appear in individual shows.

In the concluding moments of *On Your Toes* (1936), a musical satire about the then reviving Russian ballet, there took place what proved to be a far-reaching experiment— an original ballet called "Slaughter on Tenth Avenue." Seriously conceived in terms of both music (Richard Rodgers) and choreography (George Balanchine), it portrayed a tragic story of unrequited love, jealousy, and murder. Perhaps fearing to shock a pleasure-seeking Broadway audience with so red a piece of meat, the authors softened its effect by fitting the ballet into the body of the show itself as merely a play within a play. They also tagged it with a comic ending: Ray Bolger was forced to keep on dancing till he dropped, for fear of being shot by gangsters who figured in the main plot. Thus each person out front could take the ballet seriously or not, as he chose.

The experiment was successful. It showed that a Broadway audience would stand for more elevated forms of the dance than a standard tap chorus. More important, it proved that dancing, which up to that time had served chiefly as a pleasant interruption to the plot, could be employed effectively for actual storytelling. This discovery, as much as anything else, made possible the continuous dramatic flow that is the hallmark of the musical play, and without which it could not exist.

In the winter of 1940–41 two more trend-setting shows appeared: *Lady in the Dark* and *Pal Joey*. The former and commercially more successful of these dealt with a fashion-magazine editor's search for happiness through psychoanalysis. Except for Eugene O'Neill's play *Strange Interlude*, the discoveries of Freud had previously been presented on the stage chiefly in the interests of humor, with psychoanalysts generally dramatized either as boobs (*The Front Page*) or know-it-all menaces (S. N. Behrman's comedy *End of Summer*). But *Lady in the Dark* attacked the subject authentically; the author of the book, Moss Hart, is said to have checked everything with his own psychoanalyst, Dr. Gregory Zilboorg. The neurotic heroine, played by Gertrude Lawrence, went through all the usual ups and downs of life on the couch —the fears of her real life, the glories of her dream life—even to finding the key to her problem in a hidden memory of childhood. Rich in the usual elements of a successful musical—beautiful to look at, sophisticated, tuneful, amusing—*Lady in the Dark* at bottom was a serious treatment of a serious subject. As such, it added a new dimension to characterization in musicals—that of depth. Where up to that time, nearly all musical

plots had struggled with exterior problems—how to get the money, how to foil the villains, how to win the girl—*Lady in the Dark* showed that a musical could also deal successfully and fascinatingly with the inner conflicts of life.

Soon afterward, *Pal Joey* offered Broadway the story of a Chicago night-club singer who contrived to be kept in luxury by a dissolute married woman until she grew bored with his vulgarity and threw him over. Much criticized for its sordid tone, the show in its original run was not a great commercial success, despite a memorable performance by Gene Kelly in the title role. Artistically the great virtue of *Pal Joey* was its remarkable continuity. Unlike the traditional show, whose book served chiefly as a comic interlude between musical numbers little related to what preceded or followed them, *Pal Joey* was all of a piece. The songs were all "plot songs"—each not only expressed the mood of the moment but frequently pushed the story further along.

Prior to the war, then, several important departures from the old-fashioned musical comedy form had been tested and had met with success: the use of ballet to tell a story; seriousness of theme combined with depth of character; continuity of story through dialogue, song, and dance; and, finally, a general conception of the musical as a unified entertainment with all components arranged to create a collective brilliance rather than to shine individually. The stage was set for the appearance of *Oklahoma!*, *Bloomer Girl*, *On the Town*, *Carousel*, *Brigadoon*, *Kiss Me Kate*, *South Pacific*, *The King and I*, *Guys and Dolls*, *Pajama Game*, *Fanny*, *The Most Happy Fella*, *My Fair Lady*, and *New Girl in Town*.

During fifteen years these great artistic and financial successes have electrified not only Broadway but the whole country. They have changed the musical from being a show to be enjoyed and forgotten into an experience to be shared (much as a novel reader is wrapped up in his book) and remembered. A good musical play is a carefully created world in which the spectator spends an evening, and whose total effect is something more than fleeting entertainment.

There are certain penalties for this, of course. Though many musical plays are funny indeed, none of them achieves the side-splitting laughter evoked in the old days by an Ed Wynn or a Bobby Clark. Great comic per-

ORMOND GIGLI

Gwen Verdon about to partake of forbidden fruit as Eve in the ballet "Garden of Eden" in Can-Can, *1953.*

formers have no place in an integrated show; the very strength and uniqueness of their personalities would shatter its unity. All stars with high-octane personalities are in fact taboo—which is why more and more actors like Rex Harrison are turning up in musicals, while a Beatrice Lillie is rarely seen. The former can play a part; the latter must play herself.

It is also possible that the demands of the integrated show have handicapped composers. In the old days, putting together a score was principally a matter of writing half a dozen of the best songs of which one was capable when moved by the Muse, and then of grinding out an equal number to suit the dance director or the star. The latter chore often led to some remarkably bad songs; even such giants as Gershwin, Porter, Rodgers, Kern, and Berlin wrote many that sound and read like discarded entries for a Princeton Triangle Show. But the lack of restriction on the major part of the assignment resulted in dozens of songs that have remained in fashion, in some cases, for forty years and more.

Writing for an integrated show, the composer and lyric writer must closely tailor their creations to the needs of character and situation. This results in a level of quality that is very even and often high. *Kiss Me Kate* for example is, song for song, probably the best score Cole Porter ever wrote. Not one is a dud; "So In Love," "Always True to You," and one or two others are exceptional. But where is anything to equal "Night and Day," "Begin the Beguine," "I Get a Kick Out of You," or "What Is This Thing Called Love?"—all from the scores of earlier Porter shows less successful than *Kiss Me Kate?*

In a musical play it is the musical number, rather than the music itself, that people seem to remember. If the new form is often unrewarding to those who like to leave the theater whistling one of the tunes, it compensates for this by staging songs with an imagination and an effectiveness unknown twenty years ago.

One instance of this is "The Rain in Spain" in *My Fair Lady*. The scene begins with the Cockney girl Eliza laboriously repeating word-sounds pronounced for her by the phonetics professor Higgins. She improves; Higgins is cautiously hopeful. After another try she seems to have it right; Higgins is ecstatic. The music, which till then has been murmuring cautiously in the background, responds to Eliza's success by blast-

ORMOND GIGLI

Vera Zorina in George Balanchine's ballet "Slaughter on Tenth Avenue" in On Your Toes, *revived 1954.*

ing forth in a rhythmic Spanish dance while Eliza, Higgins, and Higgins' friend Colonel Pickering caper around the stage in a cockeyed parody of *Carmen*, bullfight and all, as they carol to each other the tongue twisters of speech instruction. In a musical of twenty years ago, Eliza's success probably would have been played out in dialogue alone; since the scene has no love interest or opportunity for a dance chorus, song would have been thought inappropriate. Yet "The Rain in Spain" is not only a hard-working plot song but possibly the single most delighting moment in a singularly delightful show.

An even more memorable musical-play use of song occurs at the end of the first act of *Carousel*. Having learned that his wife is to have a baby, the leading character, a carnival barker, faces the audience alone before the stage curtain. In a seven-minute solo (entitled "Soliloquy") he reacts to the news. First assuming that he will have a son, he boastfully describes all the things he will teach the boy on his way to manhood. Then it strikes him that he may instead have a daughter; the thought of her feminine defenselessness sobers him, reminding him of his own inadequacies as a provider. For a moment he sees himself for what he is—a failure. Then, with a reasoning both touching and characteristically shallow, he decides that money will solve the problem. To crashing, doom-laden chords he declares:

> *I'll go out and make it*
> *Or steal it or take it*
> *Or die!*

This not only ends the act on a powerful note of suspense but pushes the story forward into an explosive second-act situation. As "Soliloquy" proceeds, nearly a dozen musical themes—gay, boisterous, tender, lyrical, and strongly dramatic—engage the audience, each one worthy of standing as a complete song in itself. Performed without chorus or scenery, "Soliloquy" was a unique and stunning theatrical experience—in the opinion of many, one of the great moments of modern stage history.

As such examples suggest, a good musical play equates technique of presentation with the quality of the material to be sung or spoken. Musical shows have always required many talents to bring them to life—author, composer, lyricist, director, choreographer, actors, singers, dancers. In musical comedies of the old school, it was often distressingly apparent that cooks of widely

CONTINUED ON PAGE 143

THE MISSING MOURNERS OF DIJON

Compared to the question of whether Lord Elgin should have made off with the marbles of the Parthenon, the issue raised in the following article is a minor one. But it has been ruffling feathers in the art world since Mr. Auberjonois said his piece in the Toledo Blade *last spring. Americans in Europe this summer found it again in the lively new magazine* Americans Abroad, *published in Paris.*

By FERNAND AUBERJONOIS

Every year some 60,000 visitors, including quite a number of Americans, file past the tombs of the dukes of Burgundy, Philip the Bold and John the Fearless, in Dijon's celebrated Ducal Palace.

The tombs are justly regarded as true masterpieces of Gothic art. To most Burgundians they stand as symbols of a magnificent past, of a period when four knights in shining armor came close to re-creating the Holy Roman Empire and wielded considerably more power than their masters, the kings of France. And yet, as any observant sight-seer is sure to note, there is something wrong with both mausoleums.

Carved figures of Philip and John and Margaret, Philip's nagging wife, lie prone on huge slabs of black marble, hands joined in prayer, feet firmly set against the sides of benevolent lions, with angels bending over them. Beneath the noblemen and the not-so-gentle lady, master carvers of the late fourteenth and early fifteenth centuries Claus Sluter, Claus de Werve, Jean de la Huerta, and Antoine Le Moiturier set a stage for an extraordinary procession of *pleurants* (mourners).

These sixteen-inch-high alabaster statuettes were so conceived as to express human sorrow in every imaginable form under the white lacelike arcade surrounding the dukes' grave monuments. Each mourner is a perfect example of medieval statuary. There are priests, monks, members of the ducal household, choirboys—all demonstrating their grief and pain most eloquently, some with eyes turned toward the heavens, others wiping their tears on their sleeves, and some, jokingly said to be blowing their nose with their fingers, drying their heavy eyelids.

But what is wrong? Once there were eighty-two of these mourners occupying niches around the monuments. Today, several of the niches are empty. In the place of two of the statuettes a sign reading *"Au Musée de Cleveland"* informs the visitor of the fact that the occupants are now across the seas. Other signs tell him that two more monks are part of the collection of Leonard C. Hanna, also of Cleveland.

But how did they get there? And why did Paul Block, Jr., publisher of the Toledo (Ohio) *Blade*, recently call on the museum to return them to France?

To this William M. Milliken, art director of the Cleveland Museum, replied: "We will return these statuettes when the British Museum returns the Elgin Marbles to Greece and when the Toledo Museum of Art sends its Romanesque colonnades back to their original home."

THE TOLEDO Blade

These are the four missing mourners now in Cleveland. They came from the tombs of the dukes of Burgundy, seen at left in the palace at Dijon. In each empty niche there stands a small sign like the one in the picture at right which reads: "Au Musée de Cleveland."

And Paul Block: "Before this issue is resolved smoke screens are certain to be raised, involving everybody from the Greeks to the Indians. The crux of the question is, and will remain, whether or not these four small carvings are separate art treasures or whether they belong in the category of the missing arms of the Venus de Milo."

Meanwhile, Dijon stands politely and hopefully on the side lines. Will the four statuettes be given back? Or will plaster casts be made?

This reporter, having spent an afternoon overhearing comments from sight-seers who read the signs aloud, can state without hesitation that reactions from the public were, in the majority of cases, displeasure or surprise. This is natural since very few know the whole story of the missing mourners—a story that must begin at the beginning.

At the beginning we have a French nation sorely defeated by England at the Battle of Poitiers in 1356 and trying, with little success, to recover her strength. We have weak kings and powerful dukes of Burgundy, four of whom changed the face of western Europe in little over a century, establishing a string of satellite states from Switzerland to Flanders and the Zuider Zee.

In 1363, Philip the Bold was granted a handful of townships in Burgundy, and he added the rich lands in Artois and Flanders. John the Fearless defended these gains against the Duke of Orléans and was murdered in 1419, after a short and hectic reign. From 1419 to 1467, Philip the Good extended his domain to the Channel ports of Boulogne and Calais, swallowed Belgium and Luxembourg, dealt on even terms with the English, created the Order of the Golden Fleece, and dreamed of further conquests. But the dream

collapsed when Charles the Bold, who might have deserved the name of Charles the Foolhardy, provoked his Swiss neighbors and fell on the field of battle.

As death knocked at their door, two of the dukes asked that the best artisans of their time build their memorials according to specifications. Both in turn requested the carvers to picture the sorrow of courtiers at the news of the death of their leaders.

Came the Revolution and, with the uprising in provincial cities, the order from above to behead not only the living but the stone images of dead "despots." On August 8, 1795, in Dijon, when the cry of "Off with their heads" was heard, the two monuments were dismantled, the heads and hands of the statues sawed off, but the mourners were saved by a special edict from the revolutionary committee ordering the mourners to be set aside as "fairly good examples of the art of that period." Only part of the weeping little people answered a roll call in 1794. The others vanished.

Twenty-five years elapsed before an architect, Claude Saintpere, was given the task of restoring the monuments. When Saintpere finished his work, thirteen priceless Gothic statuettes were still missing. It took five of them more than a century to return to the fold.

Some of the mourners had found temporary shelter in Dijon homes. Others had covered much more territory. Thus a monk had made his way to England, where the Duke of Hamilton purchased him. A mourning choirboy became the property of an Englishman, Percy Moore-Turner, and another was purchased by the Louvre.

Four *pleurants* gathered dust in a bric-a-brac shop in Nancy until they found protectors in the persons of French collectors, who later sold them to a famous American, Clarence Mackay. At Mackay's death the statues were sold to the Cleveland Museum of Art and to Mr. Hanna.

In 1945, to the joy and delight of the people of the town, Mr. Moore-Turner donated his choirboy to the Dijon Museum. This gesture was interpreted by the Louvre as a clear hint that the companion piece, also a candelabra-carrying choirboy, should be returned. The Cluny Museum followed the excellent example set by the Louvre and gave two mourners, including the monk who had once adorned the palace of the duke of Hamilton.

Five mourners had answered the call to come home. Eight were still on the missing list. Of these, three had disappeared without leaving any trace whatsoever. One mourner is in Beaune, the property of a Mr. Perret-Carnot.

And now we come to the delicate matter of the Ohio mourners. French officials, both in Dijon and Paris, are very careful to avoid any comment that could be interpreted as criticism aimed at American collectors who, they point out, purchased the Dijon statuettes on the open market and paid considerable sums for them. But as things stand, the Dijon mourners seem to be mourning not for their dukes but for their wandering brethren in Ohio.

THE TOLEDO *Blade*

GENESIS

THE STORY OF CREATION IS SUGGESTED

BY THESE GREAT NATURE PHOTOGRAPHS

WHILE PHOTOGRAPHY IS UNIQUE IN CATCHING THE FLEETING MOMENT, SOME PHOTOGRAPHY IS GREAT IN THAT IT FIXES WHAT IT SEES IN SUCH A MANNER AS TO SUGGEST ETERNAL THINGS. THE DARKENED SUN'S MIGHTY CORONA, RECORDED AS NO HUMAN EYE COULD GLIMPSE IT, TELLS OF THE UNFATHOMED POWERS THAT BROUGHT OUR WORLD INTO BEING AND THAT GO ON MAJESTICALLY BURNING THEIR WAY THROUGH SPACE. A CAMERA PEERING INTO THE SEETHING LAVA OF A VOLCANIC CRATER SPEAKS OF THE PROCESSES OF EARTHLY FORMATION, AS DOES THE PANORAMA OF A PRIMEVAL POLAR LANDSCAPE UPON WHICH FEW MEN EVEN TO THIS DAY HAVE YET LAID EYE. AND THE PAINSTAKING PHOTOGRAPH OF SOME HUMBLE, YET LIVING THING—A LUMINOUS CREATURE IN THE WORLD OF THE SEA, THE EYE OF AN ALLIGATOR, THE TRIUMPH OF A PERFECT FRUIT AMID TENDER LEAVES—ALSO GOES ON TO TESTIFY TO THE ENDLESS MYSTERY OF CREATION.

IN THE SIXTEEN-PAGE PORTFOLIO THAT FOLLOWS, PHOTOGRAPHERS WHO HAVE USED HIGH ART IN SEARCH OF TRUTH HAVE BEEN BROUGHT TOGETHER TO BEAR WITNESS TO THE GRANDEUR OF THIS CHRONICLE. THE BURNING CRATER YOU SEE LIES IN THE BELGIAN CONGO; THE ICY LANDSCAPE IS A GREENLAND FJORD. THE SUN'S SETTING WAS SEEN IN HOLLAND, THE DEEP-BLUE CUTTLEFISH IN THE MEDITERRANEAN, THE EGG-SURROUNDED TOAD (*ALYTES OBSTETRICANS*) IN SWITZERLAND, THE REPTILIAN EYE IN A SAN FRANCISCO AQUARIUM, THE HERD OF ELEPHANTS ALONG UPLAND SLOPES IN KENYA. YET ALL BELONG TO ONE COMMON, UNIVERSAL STORY UP TO THE CREATION OF MAN HIMSELF IN THAT IMAGE ONCE SEEN BY MICHELANGELO IN THE SISTINE CHAPEL.

THESE PICTURES ARE THE WORK OF SIX PHOTOGRAPHERS: EMIL SCHULTHESS (PLATES 2, 5, 8, 9, 11); M. BRENNEISEN (PLATE 3); WERNER LÜTHY (PLATE 4); PAUL A. ZAHL (PLATE 6); OTHNAR LESNIK (PLATE 7); AND OTTO KOENIG (PLATE 10). THEY ARE REPRODUCED HERE IN A PORTFOLIO WHICH REPRESENTS THE FINEST IN GRAVURE PRINTING, EXECUTED FOR INCLUSION IN *HORIZON* BY THE SWISS FIRM OF CONZETT & HUBER, PUBLISHERS OF THE ART MAGAZINE *DU*.

In the beginning God created the heaven and the earth. . .

In the beginning God created the heaven and the earth.

2 And the earth was without form, and void; and darkness *was* upon the face
of the deep. And the Spirit of God moved upon the face of the waters.

3 And God said, Let there be light: and there was light.

4 And God saw the light, that *it was* good: and God divided the light from the
darkness.

5 And God called the light Day, and the darkness he called Night. And the
evening and the morning were the first day.

6 ¶ And God said, Let there be a firmament in the midst of the waters, and
let it divide the waters from the waters.

7 And God made the firmament, and divided the waters which *were* under
the firmament from the waters which *were* above the firmament: and it
was so.

8 And God called the firmament Heaven. And the evening and the morning
were the second day.

9 ¶ And God said, Let the waters under the heaven be gathered together unto
one place, and let the dry *land* appear: and it was so.

10 And God called the dry *land* Earth; and the gathering together of the waters
called he Seas: and God saw that *it was* good.

11 And God said, Let the earth bring forth grass, the herb yielding seed, *and*
the fruit tree yielding fruit after his kind, whose seed *is* in itself, upon the
earth: and it was so.

12 And the earth brought forth grass, *and* herb yielding seed after his kind, and
the tree yielding fruit, whose seed *was* in itself, after his kind: and God saw
that *it was* good.

13 And the evening and the morning were the third day.

14 ¶ And God said, Let there be lights in the firmament of the heaven to
divide the day from the night; and let them be for signs, and for seasons,
and for days, and years:

15 And let them be for lights in the firmament of the heaven to give light upon
the earth: and it was so.

16 And God made two great lights; the greater light to rule the day, and the
lesser light to rule the night: *he made* the stars also.

17 And God set them in the firmament of the heaven to give light upon the
earth,

18 And to rule over the day and over the night, and to divide the light from
the darkness: and God saw that *it was* good.

19 And the evening and the morning were the fourth day.

20 And God said, Let the waters bring forth abundantly the moving creature
that hath life, and fowl *that* may fly above the earth in the open firmament
of heaven.

21 And God created great whales, and every living creature that moveth,
which the waters brought forth abundantly, after their kind, and every
winged fowl after his kind: and God saw that *it was* good.

22 And God blessed them, saying, Be fruitful, and multiply, and fill the waters
in the seas, and let fowl multiply in the earth.

23 And the evening and the morning were the fifth day.

24 ¶ And God said, Let the earth bring forth the living creature after his kind,
cattle, and creeping thing, and beast of the earth after his kind: and it was so.

25 And God made the beast of the earth after his kind, and cattle after their
kind, and every thing that creepeth upon the earth after his kind: and God
saw that *it was* good.

26 ¶ And God said, Let us make man in our image, after our likeness: and let
them have dominion over the fish of the sea, and over the fowl of the air,
and over the cattle, and over all the earth, and over every creeping thing
that creepeth upon the earth.

27 So God created man in his *own* image, in the image of God created he him;
male and female created he them.

28 And God blessed them, and God said unto them, Be fruitful, and multiply,
and replenish the earth, and subdue it: and have dominion over the fish of
the sea, and over the fowl of the air, and over every living thing that moveth
upon the earth.

29 ¶ And God said, Behold, I have given you every herb bearing seed, which
is upon the face of all the earth, and every tree, in the which *is* the fruit of
a tree yielding seed; to you it shall be for meat.

30 And to every beast of the earth, and to every fowl of the air, and to every
thing that creepeth upon the earth, wherein *there is* life, *I have given* every
green herb for meat: and it was so.

31 And God saw every thing that he had made, and, behold, *it was* very good.
And the evening and the morning were the sixth day.

Thus the heavens and the earth were finished, and all the host of them.

There wanted yet the Mafter work, the end
Of all yet don; a Creature who not prone
And Brute as other Creatures, but endu'd
With Sanctitie of Reafon, might erect
His Stature, and upright with Front ferene
Govern the reft, felf-knowing, and from thence
Magnanimous to correfpond with Heav'n,
But grateful to acknowledge whence his good
Defcends, thither with heart and voice and eyes
Directed in Devotion, to adore
And worfhip God Supream, who made him chief
Of all his works : therefore the Omnipotent
Eternal Father (For where is not hee
Prefent) thus to his Son audibly fpake.
    Let us make now Man in our image, Man
In our fimilitude, and let them rule
Over the Fifh and Fowle of Sea and Aire,
Beaft of the Field, and over all the Earth,
And every creeping thing that creeps the ground.
This faid, he formd thee, *Adam*, thee O Man
Duft of the ground, and in thy noftrils breath'd
The breath of Life; in his own Image hee
Created thee, in the Image of God
Exprefs, and thou becam'ft a living Soul.

A page from Paradise Lost *by John Milton, first edition, 1669*

A detail from The Creation of Adam
by Michelangelo, in the Sistine Chapel

The Conversational Memoirs of Igor Stravinsky

Dostoyevsky and Dylan Thomas, Strauss and Proust,

and today's jazz all figure in his recollections

Born near St. Petersburg in 1882, Igor Stravinsky found himself domiciled in Hollywood last year as his seventy-fifth birthday approached, and besieged there by requests for interviews to honor the occasion. To avoid repetition and triviality and to be sure of saying what was really on his mind, he conceived an interview of his own, in collaboration with a friend and colleague of long standing, Robert Craft. Beginning with questions put to him by Craft on his methods of composition, Stravinsky gradually widened the scope of the questions to include recollections of his contemporaries, reminiscences of his early life, and his opinions on music in general. The resulting dialogue, with answers sometimes given directly in English and sometimes first cast in Russian or French on small scraps of paper, was begun in California and finished in Venice eight months later.

Since Stravinsky has moved so widely in the artistic and literary worlds of two continents over a span of three-score years and more, the range of his recollections is long and wide. This selection of them has had to forego, for instance, such touches as his boyhood memory of receiving acknowledgement of his curb-side greeting by Czar Alexander III, riding past in a droshky; of catching a glimpse of the aged Henrik Ibsen on a "delicious spring morning" in Oslo; of the ceremonious manners of the composer Moussorgsky in the home of Stravinsky's parents in St. Petersburg; of Auguste Rodin appearing, with beard and pince-nez, at a Stravinsky ballet in Paris. Only the highlights are given here of a memoir to be published in book form early next year by Doubleday & Company as Conversations with Stravinsky, *by Igor Stravinsky and Robert Craft.*

Q. From 1903 to 1906 you studied with Rimsky-Korsakov in St. Petersburg. Would you describe him as a teacher?

A. Although he was a professor at the St. Petersburg Conservatory at the time, he advised me not to enter it; instead, he made me the most precious gift of his unforgettable lessons. He gave me Beethoven piano sonatas, quartets, and his own music to orchestrate (when his own orchestrations were still unpublished). Then as I brought him my work, he showed me his own orchestra score, which he compared with mine, explaining his reasons for doing it differently. He never complimented me; he was always very close-mouthed and stingy in praising his pupils.

Q. When you were Rimsky's pupil, did you esteem Tchaikovsky as much as you did later, in the 1920's and '30's?

A. Then, as later in my life, I was annoyed by the too frequent vulgarity of his music—annoyed in the same measure as I enjoyed the real freshness of Tchaikovsky's talent and his instrumental inventiveness, especially when I compared it with the stale naturalism and amateurism of the "Five" (Borodin, Rimsky-Korsakov, Cui, Balakirev, and Moussorgsky).

Q. During your years with Rimsky-Korsakov, what opinion did you have of Moussorgsky?

A. Being influenced by the master who recomposed almost the whole work of Moussorgsky, I repeated what was usually said about his "big talent" and "poor musicianship," and about the "important services" rendered by Rimsky to his "embarrassing" and "unpresentable" scores. Very soon I realized the partiality of this kind of mind, however, and changed my attitude toward Moussorgsky.

Q. Your father and Dostoyevsky were friends. I suppose you as a child heard a great deal about Dostoyevsky.

A. Dostoyevsky became in my mind the symbol of the artist continually in need of money. My mother talked about him in this way; she said he was always grubbing. He gave readings from his own works and these were supported by my parents, although they complained that they were intolerably boring. Dostoyevsky liked music and often went to concerts with my father. Incidentally, I still consider Dostoyevsky to be the greatest Russian writer after Puskhin. Today, when one is supposed to reveal so much of oneself by one's preference for Freud or Jung, Stravinsky or Schönberg, Dostoyevsky or Tolstoi, I am a Dostoyevskyan.

Q. Were you impressed by any visiting foreign musicians in your student days in St. Petersburg?

A. Gustav Mahler impressed me greatly—the man himself and his conducting. His concert in St. Petersburg was a triumph.

Rimsky was still alive, I believe, but he wouldn't have attended because a work by Tchaikovsky was on the program.

Q. What do you recall of the composer Erik Satie?

A. He was certainly the oddest person I have ever known, but also the most rare and consistently witty person, too. I had a great liking for him and he appreciated my friendliness, I think, and liked me in return. He spoke very softly, hardly opening his mouth, but he delivered each word in an inimitable, precise way. No one ever saw him wash: he had a horror of soap. . . . Instead he was forever rubbing his fingers with pumice. He was always very poor—poor by conviction, I think. He lived in a poor section, and his neighbors seemed to appreciate his coming among them: he was greatly respected by them. His apartment was also very poor. It did not have a bed, but only a hammock. In winter Satie would fill bottles with hot water and put them flat in a row underneath his hammock.It looked like some strange kind of marimba. I don't think he knew much about instruments, and I prefer his *Socrate* as he played it for me on the piano to the clumsy orchestra score. But the real trouble with *Socrate* is that it is metrically boring. Who can stand that much regularity?

Q. What do you think of Ravel?

A. In relation to Satie he appears quite ordinary. He was dry and reserved and sometimes little darts were hidden in his remarks, but he was always a very good friend to me. He drove a truck or ambulance in the war, as you know, and I admired him for it because at his age and with his name, he could have had an easier place—or done nothing. He looked rather pathetic in his uniform; so

MOUSSORGSKY

small, he was two or three inches smaller than I am.

I think Ravel knew when he went to the hospital for his last [brain] operation that he would go to sleep for the last time. He said to me, "They can do what they want with my cranium as long as the ether works." It didn't work, however, and the poor man felt the incision. I did not visit him in the hospital, and my last view of him was at the funeral home. The top part of his skull was still bandaged. His final years were cruel, for he was gradually losing his memory and some of his coordinating powers, and he was, of course, quite aware of it. Gogol died screaming; Diaghilev died laughing; and Puccini, singing. But Ravel died gradually. That is the worst.

Q. What were Diaghilev's powers of musical judgment? What, for example, was his response to *Le Sacre du Printemps* when he first heard it? *

A. Diaghilev did not have so much a good musical judgment as he did an immense flair for recognizing the potentiality of success in a piece of music or a work of art in general. In spite of his surprise when I played him the beginning of the *Sacre* at the piano, in spite of his ironical attitude at first to its long line of repeated chords, he quickly realized that the reason for these was something other than my inability to compose more diversified music. He realized at once the seriousness of my new musical speech, its importance, and the advantage of capitalizing on it.

Q. Was the first performance of *Le Sacre du Printemps* reasonably correct? Do you recall anything more about that night of May 29, 1913, beyond what you have already written?

A. I was sitting in the fourth or fifth row on the right and the image of Monteux's back is more vivid in my mind today than the picture of the stage. He stood there apparently impervious and as nerveless as a crocodile. It is still almost incredible to me that he actually brought the orchestra through to the end. I left my seat when the heavy noise began—light noise had started from the very beginning—and went backstage behind Nijinsky in the right wing. Nijinsky

* Sergei Diaghilev, impresario of the Ballet Russe, then the leading ballet organization of the world, caused a major sensation in Paris in 1913 when he there produced in a radical departure from "classical" tradition the musically revolutionary score of Stravinsky's *Le Sacre du Printemps* ("The Rites of Spring"), with Pierre Monteux conducting and the dancer Nijinsky as choreographer. This occasion, as definitive in ballet as in the rise of modern music altogether, was marked by hostile demonstrations in the audience and by a long-protracted debate among professionals afterward as to whether or not the players had actually done what Stravinsky had expected them to do.

stood on a chair, just out of view of the audience, shouting numbers to the dancers. I wondered what on earth these numbers had to do with the music, for there are no thirteens and seventeens in the metrical scheme of the score.

From what I heard of the musical performance, it was not bad. Sixteen full rehearsals had given the orchestra at least some security. After the performance we were excited, angry, disgusted, and happy. I went with Diaghilev and Nijinsky to a restaurant. Far from weeping and reciting Pushkin in the Bois de Boulogne, as the legend is, Diaghilev's only comment was, "Exactly what I wanted." He certainly looked contented.

Q. You were a friend of Gabriele d'Annunzio's at one time, weren't you?

A. I saw rather a lot of him just before the 1914 war. I met him for the first time in

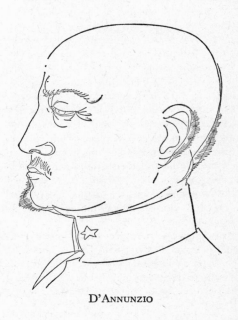

D'ANNUNZIO

Paris at Mme Golobeff's, a Russian *grande dame* of the Mme Récamier school. One day D'Annunzio entered her salon—a small man, brisk and natty, very perfumed and very bald. He was a brilliant, fast, and very amusing talker, so unlike the talk in his books. After that he came to my apartment in Paris, to the Ballet, and to concerts of mine in France and Italy. Then, suddenly, it was discovered that his execrable taste in literature went together with Mussolini's execrable taste in everything else. He was no longer a "character" and no longer amusing. But whether or not he survives as a readable author, his influence does still survive: the interiors of many Italian homes still follow descriptions in his novels.

Q. Would you describe your meeting with Claude Monet?

A. I don't know where Diaghilev found the

old man or how he managed to get him into a box at one of our Ballet Russe spectacles, but I saw him there and came to take his hand. It was after the war, in 1922 or 1923 I think, and of course no one would believe it *was* Claude Monet. He wore a white beard and was nearly blind. I know now what I wouldn't have believed then, namely, that he was painting his greatest pictures at that time—those huge, almost abstract canvases of pure color and light, ignored until recently; I believe they are in the Musée de l'Orangerie, but a very beautiful *Water Lilies*, which now looks as good as any of the period, I go to see in the Museum of Modern Art every time I am in New York.* Old Monet, hoary and near blind, couldn't have impressed me more if he had been Homer himself.

Q. While you are reminiscing, would you describe your last meeting with Proust?

A. After the *première* of my short opera *Mavra* in June, 1922, I went to a party given by a friend of mine, Princess Violette Murat, and Marcel was there also. Most of the people came to that party from my *première* at the Opera, but Proust came directly from his bed, getting up as usual very late in the evening. He was a pale man, elegantly and Frenchly dressed, wearing gloves and carrying a cane. I talked to him about music and he expressed much enthusiasm for the late Beethoven quartets—enthusiasm I certainly would have shared, were it not a commonplace among the intellectuals of that time and not a musical judgment but a literary pose.

Q. What was the subject of the opera you had planned to write with Dylan Thomas?

A. I don't think you can say that the project ever got as far as having a subject, but Dylan had a very beautiful idea. In May, 1953,

* This painting was the one work of art destroyed in a fire at the Museum of Modern Art in April of this year.

PROUST

Boston University proposed to commission me to write an opera with Dylan. I was in Boston at the time, and Dylan came to see me. As soon as I saw him, I knew that the only alternative was to love him. He was very nervous, however, chain-smoking the whole time, and he complained of severe gout pains, ". . . but I prefer the gout to the cure; I'm not going to let any doctor shove a bayonet into me twice a week." His face and skin had the color and swelling of too much drinking. He was a shorter man than I had expected from his portraits, not more than five feet five or six, with a large protuberant behind and belly. His nose was a red bulb and his brown eyes were glazed. He drank a glass of whiskey with me which made him more at ease, although he kept worrying about his wife's saying he had to hurry home to Wales "or it would be too late."

He talked to me about my *Rake's Progress* [the opera for which the poet W. H. Auden had written the libretto]. He knew the libretto well, and he admired it: "Auden is the most skillful of us all." I don't know how much he knew about music, but he talked about the operas he knew and liked and about what he wanted to do. His opera was to be about the rediscovery of our planet following an atomic misadventure. There would be a re-creation of language, only the new one would have no abstractions; there would be only people, objects, and words. He promised to avoid poetic self-indulgence: "No conceits, I'll knock them all on the head." He talked to me about Yeats, who he said was almost the greatest lyric poet since Shakespeare, and quoted from memory the poem with the refrain, "Daybreak and a candle's end." He agreed to come to visit me in Hollywood as soon as he could. Returning there, I had a room built for him, an extension from our dining

THOMAS

room, as we have no guest room. I expected a telegram from him announcing the time of arrival of his airplane. On November 9 the telegram came. It said he was dead. All I could do was to cry.

Q. Do you now admit any of the operas of Richard Strauss?

A. I would like to admit all Strauss operas to whatever purgatory punishes triumphant banality. Their musical substance is cheap and poor; it cannot interest a musician today. His now so ascendant *Ariadne auf Naxos?* I cannot bear Strauss's 6/4 chords: *Ariadne* makes me want to scream. Strauss himself? I had the opportunity to observe him closely during Diaghilev's production of his *Josephslegende* more closely than at any other time. He conducted the *première* of that work and spent some time in Paris during the preparation. He never wanted to speak German with me, though my German was better than his French. He was very tall, bald, energetic, a picture of the *bourgeois allemand*. I watched him at rehearsals, and I admired the way he conducted. His manner to the orchestra was not admirable, however, and the musicians heartily detested him. But every corrective remark he made was exact: his ears and his musicianship were impregnable.

Q. What music delights you most today?

A. I play the English virginalists with never-failing delight. I also play the Brahms-Chrysander [edition of] Couperin. Bach cantatas too numerous to distinguish, Italian madrigals even more numerous, Masses by Josquin, Okeghem, and Obrecht, are always delightful to me. Haydn quartets and symphonies, and Beethoven quartets, sonatas, and especially symphonies like his Second, Fourth, and Eighth, are sometimes wholly fresh and delightful to me. Of the music of this century I am still most attracted by two periods of Anton von Webern.* I prefer his later instrumental works and the songs he wrote after the first twelve opus numbers and before the *Trio*—music which escaped the danger of the too great preciosity of the earlier pieces, and which is perhaps the richest Webern ever wrote. People who do not share my feeling for this music will wonder at my attitude. So I explain: Webern is for me the *juste de la musique*, and I do not hesitate to shelter myself behind the protection of his not-yet-canonized art.

Q. What is your attitude to jazz?

CONTINUED ON PAGE 132

* His music, which was both nonmelodic and nonharmonic in the traditional sense, is generally considered to be the epitome of "abstract" music. It relies for its effect on the successive formation of related patterns of rhythm and tone colors. Webern also made use of Schönberg's controversial "twelve-tone" system as against the conventional Western eight-note scale.

ILLUSTRATED FOR HORIZON BY EUGENE KARLIN

"Great is Diana of the Ephesians"

The ruins of her ancient capital

yield the finest statue yet found

of the "Mother Goddess of Asia"

The ancient Greeks were always ready to incorporate strange gods into their own household of divinities. When they colonized Ephesus in Asia Minor in about 1000 B.C., they found a primeval eastern goddess of motherhood and fertility being worshiped, whom they soon blended with their own Artemis—the Roman Diana. To her the Ephesians built the great temple housing her towering image that became a wonder of the classic world. Temple and image were later destroyed; but this life-sized marble representation, carved in Roman times and recently found by the Austrian Institute of Archaeology, is thought by its finders to be the closest known approach to the original, and certainly the most splendid.

While the Ephesian Artemis has long been called "the many-breasted Mother of Asia," Dr. Franz Miltner, discoverer of this figure, holds that what is actually represented on her bosom is a bodice spangled with eggs. "The many animal figures (rams, lions, hinds, griffins, and sphinxes) that decorate her robe symbolize her power over all nature. The signs of the zodiac on her breast also point to her power over the heavens. Young and stately, she is the life-giving and life-preserving mistress of the cosmos."

When Saint Paul tried to convert her city to Christianity, he was resisted by devotees who "all with one voice about the space of two hours cried out, Great is Diana of the Ephesians." Yet, perhaps at the end of the fourth century A. D., this image of her was buried away, along with the last survivals of her cult.

On the following page:
an article on Ephesus
by Freya Stark

REPRINTED FROM *The Loom of History* BY HERBERT J. MULLER (HARPER & BROTHERS); COURTESY OF THE TURKISH GOVERNMENT

Croesus and other ancient monarchs marched along the Sacred Way of Ephesus that led to Diana's temple.

Timeless Home of the Mother Goddess

Seat of one of the Seven Wonders of the ancient world,

Ephesus has known three millennia of changing culture

The statue of Artemis lately dug up in Ephesus and shown on the preceding page has little enough in common with the slim huntress of the Greeks. She was worshiped there before the Ionians came. Clustered about with the heads of her deer and her lions, the ancient Mother Goddess of Asia looks into space with that impersonal divinity, a benevolence free of compassion, which the Christian ideal of kindness was soon to humanize in the world where the statue was carved.

Yet in Ephesus, whose Roman age is now being disinterred, the Mother Goddess survived; the Virgin Mary's first church was dedicated there, and its pilasters stand today; and even now, high up, beyond the pagan walls of Lysimachus, a new center of worship is growing, dedicated to the place where a German nun in a vision saw the dormition of the Mother of God.

The ages pursue each other, and answers are better or worse according to the hearts and minds that find them. But the questions asked are more or less the same, and there is no place so adapted to the development of the historical sense as a center of ancient pilgrimage that still continues to worship. Through the study of many vicissitudes and different faiths, toleration and humility are encouraged—perhaps our most essential necessities on the edge of the nuclear world.

This is brought home particularly by the fact that the Ephesus now being excavated is the one most familiar to our own age. The earliest traditions of this city are lost in the haze of Ionia, rich and luminous as its climate, but vague. Some said it was founded by the Amazons, and some by the Leleges and Carians, who in their thin lives invented goddesses of enormous fatness and ran their small boats in and out of the Aegean coasts and islands before the Greeks came or the age of iron had entered into that of bronze. The colonizers arrived and mixed with these people, landing from Attica, according to the legend, under the leadership of Androclus, son of Codrus, the Athenian king. Centuries later, in the days of the chronicler Strabo, the descendants

By FREYA STARK

of this family were still called kings and sat in honorable front seats at the games, wearing purple robes and a staff in the place of a scepter, and superintended the sacrifices to the Eleusinian Demeter. Under this joint habitation and mixed worship, the city prospered. When Croesus of Lydia invaded it, the citizens tied their walls to the temple, nearly a mile away, dedicated themselves to their goddess, and were spared.

Soon after these events, the town itself moved from its earliest hilltop and settled around the temple, which grew in splendor almost into the age of Alexander. On the night of Alexander's birth, according to tradition, a madman named Herostratus set the temple on fire; enamored of publicity like many a later destroyer, he thought out this way of making his name remembered, and succeeded. The temple lay in ruins when the young conqueror, after his first victory in Asia, came marching down from the river Granicus to the Grecian cities of the coast, and offered to rebuild it at his own expense if the citizens would acknowledge him as its founder.

Alexander was so poor at the time that he very soon afterward had to disband his navy temporarily, so it was perhaps as well that the citizens refused. The rich contributed their property and the women their jewels, and the new temple, built by the Ephesians themselves, was counted as one of the Seven Wonders of the World. Of its pillars, sixty feet in height and 127 in number, "everyone the offering of a king," a few fragments and a base are in the British Museum; but the works of the great sculptors Praxiteles and Scopas, the picture of the most famous painter, Apelles, in which Alexander appeared armed with thunder, the doors of cypress, the roof of cedar, the steps of vine—all have vanished. The very shape of the great building is unknown, and the wooden image of the goddess, said to have descended from Zeus, adorned with embroidered robes and preserved in nard or some other oily substance through all the city's revolutions, was presumably burned. But the worship was renewed, with its virgin priestesses and eunuch priests, and the holy month continued to be kept for its service. The right of sanctuary attached to the temple was extended by Alexander and Mithridates the Great and further enlarged by Mark Antony, until the administrative realism of the Emperor Augustus abolished it altogether because of the malefactors who were able to find a refuge in the shadow of the shrine.

With this we come into the Roman age, which began in Asia Minor in 190 B.C. with the battle of Magnesia. There Antiochus the Great, descended from one of Alexander's generals, was defeated not far from Ephesus, across the range of Tmolus to the north. I have driven five miles

In the Christian Era, the Ephesian cult of Artemis gave way to worship of Mary, the Mother of God, whom many believed to have been buried within their city walls. This statue was found among ruins.

or so from Ephesus toward the site into the Caÿster valley—the Little Menderes, the Turkish inhabitants now call it—to look for Homer's wild swans in marshes that gave their name to the continent of Asia.

> *and as about the flood*
> *Caïster, in an Asian mead, flocks of the airy brood,*
> *Cranes, geese, or long-necked swans, here, there, proud of*
> *their pinions fly,*
> *And in their falls lay out such throats, that with their*
> *spiritful cry*
> *The meadow shrieks again; so here, these many-nationed men*
> *Flowed over the Scamandrian field . . .*

It was April when I drove there by a narrow dusty road. The marshy lake shimmered through trees beside it, covered, as if bright carpets had been laid upon it, with reeds and lilies and sheets of yellow water flowers. In the village lands behind, the fig trees and the mulberries too were bright and luscious, and Judas trees and syringa were in blossom. The banks of the road were thick with flowers—poppies wrinkled like dried blood, the last asphodels yellow or pale, and many vetches; daisies and the sophisticated, honey-scented grape hyacinth in clusters. The hillsides, uninhabited but easy, sloped down under their olives, each tree a separate light and shadow of its own. And here in this sheltered solitude the water birds cried and nested. Whether they were swans or not I could not see, and some were black and certainly coot, and some were more like cormorant; but they were there in crowds stretching their necks

CONTINUED ON PAGE 140

87

NOT A PALACE

This new pharmaceuticals plant, with a carport to the left and laboratory and office space on the right, stands beside a busy four-lane highway in Pasadena. Company owner Arthur Hanisch gave free rein to architect Edward D. Stone (above), whose original, luxurious treatment, making dramatic use of grill-work, won a top American Institute of Architects award. Left, President Hanisch on the balcony of his plant's central, covered courtyard or atrium.

BUT A PILL FACTORY

Pasadena this year saw the building of a factory which many Californians consider the most beautiful commercial building in the world. No one was more surprised by its looks than the man who ordered and paid for it.

Several years ago President Arthur Hanisch of the Stuart Company, a small and prospering pharmaceuticals firm, decided he needed a new combination plant and office building for his 160 employees. He had two ideas, eloquent in their simplicity: first, to get the most brilliant architect he could find to design it for him, and second, to give that architect entirely free rein—even to the point of refusing to go and look at the building until it was finished.

Edward D. Stone of New York, the man Hanisch chose, was fresh from planning the spacious new United States Embassy at New Delhi in an idiom of grillwork and columns of his own. He had won fame for many showpiece residences and major institutional buildings beginning with New

York's Museum of Modern Art in 1939. But he had done comparatively little commercial architecture before Hanisch came to him, asking for something that would be not only efficient but beautiful and luxurious as well. What Stone produced left his client breathless on first laying eyes on it, and stunned the Stuart Company's employees too. "It's out of this world," exclaimed Hanisch; "I knew it'd be beautiful, but not *that* beautiful."

With three acres and $2,000,000 at his disposal, the architect laid out a long, low structure deeply set back amid greenery and reflecting pools and uniquely combining the elements of contemporary-style cantilevers, arabesque grilles, and a central Roman atrium, or covered inner court. Fountains, ferns, palms, Asiatic sculpture round out the décor. Inside, although you might not think so at first glance, pills are made.

The pill, a humble although vital object, does not demand

89

Executives work behind the grillwork that screens the plant from outside.

Palms, fountains, reflecting pools, and greenery inside and out add a touch of exotic fantasy to the Pasadena pill maker's headquarters. Yet despite its architectural exuberance, the building is planned to be a coolly efficient manufacturing center. The theory behind it is that aesthetic appeal will help and not hinder its work.

Edward D. Stone holds patent rights on his Orient-inspired grille designs.

One way of designing a factory corridor. Offices are beyond.

large machinery for its production, but it does call for utter cleanliness, precision, and alertness of supervision. Around Arthur Hanisch's atrium are grouped air-conditioned laboratories and shops in which his employees work under diffused lighting and acoustical ceilings at machines finished in a soft tone that the company calls "Stuart Blue." Coming off the job, they take their meals shoulder to shoulder with company executives in the atrium's dining space under huge gilded saucers filled with greenery and hanging mother-of-pearl globes that shimmer like Japanese lanterns. A swimming pool and 30,000-square-foot recreation center are also on hand to help the Stuart workers and their families relax.

"All I had to do was to find the right talent," is Hanisch's comment. "Giving freedom to an architect is bound to result in a better job." In this case it has resulted also in a blow to the common idea that a handsome commercial building necessarily costs more than an ugly one. President Hanisch estimates that his method of giving Stone full control over all elements of the design saved him about $13 per square foot as against what a conventionally designed structure might have cost. And, speaking of operating economies, he adds, "All this beauty is saving me a lot of money—about $700,000 this year. But does that make the beauty any less beautiful?" Whatever the actual economics, the client got a show place and the employees a near country club that may inspire their fellows in other plants to rear their heads and look for something comparable.

"If we can persuade industrialists and businessmen that they can have buildings and factories that do not sacrifice the least bit of usefulness and yet can be aesthetically pleasing, we can change the shape of the world," is Edward Stone's comment on his own aim. And this ideal of a new order in commercial architecture is one he shares with an increasing number of colleagues. Across the country, the firm of Skidmore, Owings & Merrill recently designed for the Connecticut General Life Insurance Company a building comparable in spirit to Stone's in Pasadena, although on a far larger scale. On a site of 268 rolling acres in Bloomfield, Connecticut, they laid out a long, low complex of offices with glass and metal exterior walls in a setting of gardens, sunken plazas, lines of trees, sculpture, and pools. For this they won a top award in the 1958 best-design competition sponsored by the American Institute of Architects, while Stone's also took top honors.

The Stuart Company's President Hanisch started his working life as a hand in a dreary canning factory. Evidently he did not want to be even the head of a dreary factory. Something of the expansiveness and exuberance that marks the West Coast got into his bones, and certainly into those of Stone, too. As for his employees, they are reportedly content—as well they may be. "This isn't Hollywood," remarked one visitor recently. "It's just Utopia."

Around the world with Stone's grilles

The grille motif used by architect Stone in the Pasadena factory (opposite) has been applied so widely by him as to become virtually his trade-mark. Above, from top: his United States pavilion at this year's Brussels Exposition; the recent residence designed for Bruno Graf in Dallas, Texas; the U. S. Embassy Chancellery at New Delhi. In the Graf residence, an indoor pool surrounds the dining room.

By IRVING STONE

The Perfect Beauty

Beloved of prince and painter, Simonetta Vespucci was the Renaissance ideal

She was born at Porto Venere, near Genoa, precisely where the Italians believe Venus to have emerged from the blue waters after her birth in the Mediterranean. At her death at the age of twenty-two the city of Florence went into mourning, following her funeral train from the Palazzo Vespucci to the Church of the Ognissanti. She lay in state while men and women alike walked past her bier with tears streaming unashamedly down their cheeks as they gazed for the last time at her long, silken textured honey-copper hair, the gold over fresh cream skin, remembering the wide-set, radiant and yet tender eyes, the features sculptured with the flawless symmetry of Donatello's living marble.

Lorenzo the Magnificent said, "Her manners were so sweet and attractive that she gave everybody who was familiar with her the absolute certainty that she loved him. It seemed impossible that she was loved by so many men without any jealousy and praised by so many women without envy."

Who was Simonetta Vespucci, who could arouse such adoration among the beauty-drenched Florentines, and today, almost five hundred years later, still causes men to fall in love with her at first breath-taking sight?

The facts of her life are few, simple, and obscured in the mists of romantic literature. She was born Simonetta Cattaneo in 1453, of an old and noble Genoese family. Though their wealth was on the decline there was still enough money for her mother, Cattocchia di Marco Spinola, to travel frequently throughout Italy, where she was connected by ties of blood and friendship with many of the great houses of Tuscany, including that of the ruling Medici.

It was when Simonetta had just turned sixteen that her mother betrothed her to Marco Vespucci. The Vespucci had been leaders of Florentine political life and trade since the fourteenth century, in the same social strata as the Pitti, Strozzi, Pazzi, and Tornabuoni families. Their relationship with the Medici went back to the founder of that dynasty; they were still not only intimate friends but business partners in world commerce and banking.

Because of the decline in the Cattaneo fortunes, Cattocchia had to be content with a member of one of the lesser branches of the Vespucci as her daughter's betrothed. Sixteen-year-old Marco was the son of a seafaring father who at one time was in command of the Florentine galleys voyaging from Pisa to Barbary and Syria. A relative, Jacopo d'Appiano, ruler of Piombino, provided Simonetta's dowry, "a certain quantity of iron from the mines" at Piombino.

Simonetta and Marco had never met. Around August of 1469 Marco and his family arrived in Genoa, where the wedding ceremony was performed. It was a good marriage for Simonetta, in Florentine terms, where the family into which one married was more important than the appearance or the character of the bridegroom. The young newlyweds then started south for Florence, home of the greatest painters, sculptors, poets, and humanists amid the rebirth of Greek culture and the birth of the modern world.

Each branch of the Vespucci family had a palace in the Borgo d'Ognissanti, close to the Porta al Prato through which they brought in the wine from their estates. Simonetta moved into one of the lesser Vespucci palaces, with the family coat of arms above the door, living with Marco's parents and his sister Bice, next-palace to her new cousin Amerigo Vespucci. Two years older than herself and Marco, Amerigo was to continue the explorations of the New World begun by Christopher Columbus, Simonetta's fellow-Genoese.

Simonetta could have been expected to settle down to

The beauty of Simonetta Vespucci is immortalized in this portrait by Piero di Cosimo. Though painted some years after she died, it bears her name and represents the Florentine ideal of feminine beauty which she embodied. Simonetta was twenty-two when she died. The snake around her neck is intended to symbolize her tuberculosis and perhaps also to link her with the great beauty of antiquity, Cleopatra.

the anonymous life of an aristocratic Florentine wife, bearing numerous children, plying her needle on the open loggia penthouse in warm weather, amusing herself at the colorful processions, tournaments, and receptions with which Lorenzo the Magnificent kept the pleasure-mad Florentines entertained. And so she might have, had not two men fallen in love with her. The first, of her own age, was Giuliano de'Medici, handsome and dashing younger brother of Lorenzo, coinheritor of the incredible wealth, power, talent, and wisdom of the Medici dynasty. The second was a penniless and friendless artist, Sandro Botticelli, son of a tanner and nine years her senior. Without Simonetta's face to glow in his pictures, Botticelli might well have remained little more than a magnificent technician like his contemporary Ghirlandaio. Without Botticelli to paint her, Simonetta might have emerged as an interesting footnote in the turbulent history of the Medici.

Together Botticelli and Simonetta immortalized each other. Today it is to the lonely and unloved Botticelli that she belongs, rather than to her husband, Marco Vespucci, or her prince-gallant, Giuliano de' Medici.

On January 28, 1475, twenty-one-year-old Giuliano de' Medici staged a spectacular tournament in the Piazza Santa Croce. It is reputed to have eclipsed in splendor even that of

Botticelli's Venus is the image of Simonetta, which lived on in the painter's mind long after she died.

Lorenzo of 1469. The nobility of all Europe was invited. The youths of the noblest families entered the jousts, dressed in brilliant silks adorned with pearls and rubies. Giuliano's silver armor and velvet mantle cost eight thousand gold florins. Each contestant was backed by twenty young men in jeweled armor made by Florence's world-famous goldsmiths, and followed by a full troop of soldiers. Each cavalier carried a banner on which had been painted, by such artists as Verrocchio, the lady of his love.

Giuliano called in Botticelli to paint the exquisite Simonetta on his banner. It was the only time that she was ever painted from life. Botticelli conceived her as Pallas, the fully-armed goddess of wisdom; she wore "a dress of fine gold down to her knees, and under that a white gown shaded with golden powder, a pair of azure half boots, standing with her feet upon two flames of fire, in a meadow full of flowers . . ."

The twin climax of the pageantry came when Giuliano, not unexpectedly, was acclaimed champion of his own tournament, and Simonetta was crowned Queen of Beauty to the roared approval of the entire population of Florence.

In a box of honor at the side of the piazza sat Marco, surrounded by collateral Vespucci and watching his wife being honored by a Medici who was obviously in love with her. We have no portrait of Marco, for the alleged portrait of him in the Vespucci Chapel of the Ognissanti, painted by Ghirlandaio, has been proven to be that of another, more important Vespucci. He was a quiet young man, blessed with no particular talent or ambition, working without distinction in the Vespucci wine and silk business. But he had a temper; he could grow embittered; he fought back when he thought his rights were being violated.

Was Giuliano Simonetta's lover? The original charge to this effect was made in a long poem by Poliziano, most brilliant of the humanists in Lorenzo's Platonic Academy, "*La Giostra di Giuliano de' Medici*," written after Simonetta's death and telling the story of the tournament. Here Poliziano calls Simonetta Giuliano's mistress. Vasari, bad painter but excellent biographer of the Renaissance artists, who was born thirty-five years later, in turn labeled Simonetta Giuliano's *innamorata*, and generations of art historians have repeated the assumption.

Was Simonetta chaste? The women of Florence, with whom she spent her days and who might well have hated her for her matchless beauty, thought so. The old men warming themselves in the early morning sun on the benches before the *palazzi* knew everything that had transpired during the night; by sundown their transmission would have covered the whole valley of the Arno.

The documents of the period are voluminous, for the Florentines were inveterate letter and journal writers. From the hundreds still existing we know precisely to whom everyone was making love, there being no tidbit the Floren-

The image of Simonetta inspired Botticelli's brush when he painted La Primavera: *she is not only Venus but the flower-decked spirit of Spring and the Three Graces as well. Her spirit pervades the whole painting, with its feeling of sadness at the transience of youthful beauty.*

tines more enjoyed setting down. But no syllable about Simonetta is to be found, in letter or journal, during her lifetime or after her death, that suggests infidelity.

The Vespucci loved and respected her; her father-in-law expressed the deepest affection for her; she was buried in the Vespucci vault with full honors. It was not in the character of the Vespucci family to take in silence a public cuckolding, to allow Florence to call one of them the ugliest word in the Italian language, *cornuto*, with the first and little finger extended upward to symbolize horns.

Lorenzo, who ruled both his family and all Florence, well knew the danger of outraging the wealthy and powerful Vespucci clan. The Florentines could drive him out any time they pleased, as was demonstrated just three years after Giuliano's tournament when the Pazzi family, prompted by Pope Sixtus IV, rose in conspiracy and stabbed Giuliano to death during a High Mass in the Duomo, almost killing Lorenzo as well. Two years after Lorenzo's death the Florentines, disliking the arrogance of Lorenzo's son Piero, sacked the Medici Palace and drove the family into exile.

That Giuliano was in love with Simonetta there can be no doubt, nor does his fathering of an illegitimate son, the later Pope Clement VII, permit any denial of his carnal

Florentine nature. But this was also the heyday of extolling Dante's idyllic love for Beatrice, Petrarch's for Laura. The lusty Florentines were not averse to a poetic passion.

Even Vasari contradicts himself when he writes, "Simonetta was virtuous and chaste. Giuliano was madly in love with her. She returned his love, but their love was pure, Platonic love at that time being the nature of the intercourse between many young Florentine lovers."

Is it important to establish Simonetta's character? Much as we may admire the linear beauty of Botticelli's paintings, it is difficult to love reverentially the image of an adulteress. The purity of Simonetta is implicit in her beauty. Take away that goodness and what remains is an exquisite mask, or, changing the figure of speech, the shell on which the Venus emerges. One can long for Simonetta, but never lust for her. Was Sandro Botticelli, who was never known to love any woman of the world, nor to be loved, perhaps projecting in paint every man's mother image, even as Michelangelo carved her in the marble of the *Pietà?*

The historians tell us that the poets of the time wrote long stanzas about Simonetta, that the painters painted her. Nothing could be farther from the truth. The poetry came after her lifetime, as did the portraits. Except for the por-

CONTINUED ON PAGE 142

The image of Johann Wolfgang von Goethe, poet and humanist as well as man of public affairs, has influenced Board Chairman Paepcke of the Container Corporation of America, who wants to see businessmen broaden themselves by ties with the humanities. For the past ten years Paepcke has been developing a unique cultural center for them at Aspen, Colorado. Its first notable occasion: a bicentenary celebration honoring Goethe.

The World of Walter Paepcke

At a "modern Weimar" high in the Rockies, a Chicago industrialist

exposes his fellow businessmen to Aristotle, Haydn, and hydrotherapy

By MARQUIS W. CHILDS

In the entrance hall of the Walter Paepckes' house in Aspen, Colorado, stands a Zuni Indian effigy that appears at first glance to be the work of a contemporary artist. It has the naïveté and the impudence of a fairly late Picasso, and in its way it might be regarded as symbolic of Aspen. For in the experiment launched high on the western slope of the Rockies by industrialist Walter P. Paepcke, the lines are curiously blurred between the old and the new, the primitive and the modern, the sophisticated and the innocent. The mixture is as heady as the clear thin air in which the snow-topped mountains look so close at hand.

Many European industrialists cultivate the humanities. They collect Klee and Kandinsky, they read Camus and William Faulkner. But this is their private life. In wanting to share his cultivation, to spread it, to organize it, to make it grow and expand, Paepcke is singularly American. At his Institute for Humanistic Studies at Aspen, he puts a dozen or more business executives around a conference table to discuss Plato and Adam Smith and Karl Marx at the prodding of a peckish professor. He sends them to a Health Center where they are put through all kinds of jerks and jumps, heated up to 180 degrees in a Finnish sauna, doused in ice water, and then turned over to masseurs who pound them with hands of steel. For this they, or their companies,

Sessions at Aspen's Institute for Humanistic Studies are strenuous two-week seminars on classic and modern theorems. Here moderator Mortimer J. Adler and poet-critic Mark van Doren meet a local press representative after conducting executives over Socratic hurdles.

SUZANNE SZASZ

Working out
on a
high level

On the principle of a sound mind in a sound body, the institute also subjects its visitors' physiques to exercises that may either leave them breathless at 7,000 feet or in unaccustomed posture.

pay $600 for a fortnight's "course," with $250 additional if the executive brings his wife. And besides the seminars and exercises, the executive still on his feet can take in the concerts provided by the annual Aspen Music Festival founded by Paepcke with its own school and resident orchestra. He can attend public lectures on subjects ranging from the newest theory in physics to the plays of Samuel Beckett. At intervals there are star turns such as an annual conference of designers that draws participants from all over the United States and abroad.

That, roughly, is the Aspen idea as evolved by Paepcke. As one European remarked upon observing this American phenomenon, "Imagine the chairman of Schneider-Creusot or a director of Barclay's bank submitting to all that!" Discussing his experiment in spreading the humanities

among businessmen, Paepcke frequently drops the expression "cross-fertilization." When he first came to Aspen in 1945, he himself had been thoroughly cross-fertilized. Then forty-nine, he was a conspicuous success in business as president of the Container Corporation of America, which had had a phenomenal growth in the packaging industry. At the same time in his native Chicago he had encountered that brilliant gadfly of American education, Robert M. Hutchins, and his acolyte, Mortimer J. Adler. Giving forth ideas as a Fourth of July pin wheel showers sparks, Hutchins attracted and interested Paepcke. Adler's "Great Books" course seemed to promise a broadening and deepening of the cultural shallows. Thus the cross-fertilization began.

Paepcke's first sight of Aspen came while he was searching for a new interest with the restless energy that marks

Full tone
near the
timber line

Now independent of founder-patron Paepcke, the Music Associates of Aspen conduct their own summer festival, attracting top soloists.

Resident composers and teachers, a music school, and a full orchestra enlarge the scope of the Associates' work, which ranges from studying and performing old and often little-known music to experimenting with the very newest. Two Aspen regulars are the pianist Victor Babin and the composer Darius Milhaud, below.

Robert M. Hutchins, perennial proponent of new educational causes, was an early backer of the Aspen idea. Below, labor leader Walter P. Reuther plunges into the debate of philosophers and businessmen in their retreat.

Seminar at work: around an octagonal table in an octagonal room hung with contemporary art, "Great Books" are discussed. Third from the left, Adler; fourth from right, William Benton.

his temperament. It was with no other motive than curiosity that the Paepckes drove from their ranch near Colorado Springs to see the old mining town that had served during the war as the center of a ski-troop training area. They were immediately taken with the mountain setting and the old town, half abandoned, with traces of the Victorian elegance of the silver bonanza of 1879 still visible in the fading splendors of the Jerome Hotel and the Opera House. The nearby slopes looked as though they had been modeled by a ski instructor. With the great increase in airplane travel certain to come with the end of the war, Aspen would attract skiers from both coasts. But Aspen even in Paepcke's first vision was to be far more than a ski resort. It was to be a new Salzburg for music. And beyond this dawned the perspective of a meeting place for the free play of ideas, a Magic Mountain that would attract the best minds in the arts and the sciences. In short, here was to be another Renaissance, with Paepcke as Medici in chief.

To a remarkable degree, that vision is by way of becoming reality. Paepcke and a few associates bought up a considerable part of the town. First came the ski resort, today equipped with the longest ski lift in the world. This was a successful business venture, as Paepcke had been certain it would be. The next phase, bringing culture to the mountain, was more difficult. Music, the gentlest of the Muses, prepared the way. Financed chiefly by Paepcke, a music school and a concert series began almost from the first to attract musicians and composers. A tent designed by Eero Saarinen was put up in Roaring Fork Valley to hold an audience of 2,000. The scraping of cellos and the tootling

TEXT CONTINUED ON PAGE 102

While Aspen streets resound to a cacophony of singers, flutists, and brass sections practicing in lofts above garages, some musicians like the Juilliard Quartet take to the open, astonishing upland cattle.

Director of the annual music festival is the conductor and teacher Izler Solomon.

1. OPERA HOUSE   6. MARBLE GARDEN

2. HOTEL JEROME   7. ASPEN MEADOW

3. MUSIC TENT   8. HEALTH CENTER

4. SEMINAR BUILDING   9. GUEST CENTER

5. VICTORIAN HOUSE   10. SKI LIFT

TEXT CONTINUED FROM PAGE 99

of flutes came from every open window along Main Street as teachers settled down for the summer.

In 1949 Paepcke succeeded in making a great many Americans aware of Aspen who had never heard of it before. He did this by dramatizing the bicentennial of Goethe's birth. To mount an observance of the occasion had originally been Hutchins' idea. But where? Why not, said Paepcke, relate the poet of Germany's renaissance to the rebirth of Aspen?

Paepcke, as a director of the Goethe Bicentennial Foundation, had the shrewd idea of bringing Albert Schweitzer to America to deliver the anniversary address. Up to that time Schweitzer had been little more than a name in this country. Something was known of his humanitarian work

BERKO-PIX

Herbert Bayer, creator of the panorama on the preceding spread, is also the architect who designed this building of concrete and tile. The letters HC stand for "Health Center"—Paepcke's retreat for executives' physical rehabilitation. Here, barefoot and dressed in sky-blue gym suits, they are put through Swedish exercises, pummeled by Austrian masseurs, then plunged into Finnish steambaths, from which they pass into "recovery rooms" and a library where they may play good music and read the hundred "Great Books."

at his hospital at Lambaréné in French Equatorial Africa. But few Americans knew of his great reputation as a philosopher, and as an organist in the exposition of the works of Bach. This was quickly corrected. The elderly philosopher's arrival in New York drew something of the attention accorded a famous film star, and his lecture at Aspen was a national event. With figures like Ortega y Gasset and G. A. Borghese also brought in for the occasion, along with the Minneapolis Symphony, culture flowered in the Rockies.

But for Paepcke something more than promotion of the humanities or even the commercial and artistic success of Aspen was involved in the Goethe celebration and Schweitzer's visit. Like many other Americans of German origin

who cherished their cultural heritage, he had been deeply affronted by Hitler and the tragic folly of the German people in following him. Here was an opportunity to show the noble side of the German character, together with the vast cultivation of Schweitzer and his profound humanity in giving up everything he loved in Europe to devote himself to the medical care of the simple African, and all this against a background of the glories of Goethe.

In any discussion of ethnic backgrounds, the German-American is usually identified with the stubborn core of American isolationism in the Midwest. But there have also been many Germans who brought with them a broad allegiance to a great cultural tradition built in the nineteenth century. They were among the first to support symphony orchestras and lecture series. From this background came Paepcke, solidly based in the prosperous upper middle class of Chicago. After Yale, where he made Phi Beta Kappa, he returned home to enter the family business, the Chicago Mill & Lumber Company, from which he later moved over to the Container Corporation.

For a man who was to harbor the ambition of starting a renaissance of the arts and letters, Paepcke chose the ideal wife. It is conceivable that the Aspen experiment would never have happened if in 1922 he had not married Elizabeth Nitze. Her father was Professor William A. Nitze, one of the many scholars attracted to the University of Chicago as it was developed with Rockefeller millions. A philologist specializing in the Romance languages, he was a broadly cultivated man. His household was a center of the cultural life of both town and gown, and its roots lay in the solid Germanic tradition of Bach, Beethoven, and Brahms. If you could imagine something of the stability of the early phase of Thomas Mann's great family chronicle, *Buddenbrooks*, transplanted to a big, comfortable house on Chicago's South Side near the university, you would have an approximation of the atmosphere in which Elizabeth Nitze grew up.

Soon the young Paepckes were taking a prominent part in the cultural community that is a small nucleus in that sprawling city. But it was not until young Robert Hutchins came to Chicago, an event compared by some historians with the Chicago fire, that the process of cross-fertilization really began. At thirty, Hutchins, who had been dean of the Yale Law School, was made president of the University of Chicago. For the next fifteen years the university was to shake and shiver as Hutchins proceeded to try out his startling ideas about higher education in America. Violent controversies arose over football, of which Hutchins disapproved, and Thomism as a philosophic force in education, of which Hutchins approved.

Through all his controversies, personal and public, the Paepckes remained loyal to their friend Hutchins. One of the things Hutchins does to friend and foe alike is to stir in them a divine discontent, and that is what happened to

Paepcke, who had begun to look with increasing restlessness beyond the horizon of his successful business.

He had already been marriage broker for a successful wedding of art and industry. During the war the Container Corporation had sponsored a series of advertisements of high artistic quality that celebrated the United Nations and only incidentally the corporation's boxes. With the end of the war, Paepcke projected a four-year series on the forty-eight states, the territories, and the District of Columbia. Paintings by indigenous artists were commissioned for it, in many instances with striking results. Peter Nielson, an Alaskan Indian whose ancestors made totem poles, did the painting on Alaska, using the totem motifs. A Hopi Indian, Fred Kabotie, was commissioned to do Arizona. Refusing to submit preliminary sketches, he went out into the desert, shot a mule deer, skinned it, painted a picture on the hide, and sent it off. Paepcke hung the painted hide complete with head and tail on the wall of his office.

A second series of advertisements, in which the corporation name appeared only in small type at the bottom, celebrated the "Great Ideas of Western Man," drawn from Mortimer Adler's "Great Books." Given a sentence or a short paragraph from Montaigne, Jefferson, Kant, or Emerson, a well-known artist was left free to interpret it as he saw fit. The result was an artistic achievement far above the standard of advertising up to that time.

One of Paepcke's deepest concerns is the isolation of the American businessman from the intellectual and cultural currents of his time. The businessman, in Paepcke's view, fails to understand how vital a part he has to play in sustaining and carrying forward the great tradition of free inquiry. Here lay the genesis of the Aspen Institute for Humanistic Studies, set up with the "Great Ideas" theme as a base, and with the object of bringing about among leading executives a realization of the obligation, the excitement, and the opportunity this inquiry implied.

In two weeks' time, the visitors were to be cross-fertilized in a concentrated fashion and brought to a sudden, sharp awareness of all that lies beyond the boundaries of getting and spending. The institute was designed around two-hour discussion periods, evening lectures, and a formidable order of outside reading ranging from Aristotle through Locke, J. S. Mill, and De Tocqueville down to Adler himself and his concept of dynamic contemporary capitalism. The exec-

CONTINUED ON PAGE 133

While trippers and motel keepers have also discovered the new Salzburg of the West and thrown up trailer camps and maudlin cabins, the land around Aspen is so vast that the hand of man still makes but little impression on it. The wide-open terrain has inspired some original architecture, such as this studio built by Herbert Bayer for himself on rugged Red Mountain. Austrian-born and trained at the German Bauhaus school, Bayer has become Walter Paepcke's chief designer both for Aspen and the huge Container Corporation.

The Perils of Drink

A shocking exposé of "fraud, adulteration, and sorcery"

in the wine cellars—and a proposal to revive the ancient medieval punishments

By RAYMOND POSTGATE

This is a grave and important article, written because I am in a grave and important mood. I think I have been poisoned, and I want somebody punished for it. I should not trouble you with this small personal matter, if it were not that I think all of us are being poisoned, more or less, and we all ought to do something about it. I mean "poisoned" in the colloquial sense; we are not being literally killed outright. If there is provably lethal material in anything that we are given to eat or drink, the authorities will interfere, or can be persuaded to do so. But we can safely be made rather ill, and kept generally below par and miserable, by food and drink that are just of poor quality. The Middle Ages did not have analytical chemists, but they knew how to tell thin ale, sawdust-like bread, and low-grade butter. And they had some choice punishments to mete out to their perpetrators. I am wondering whether some of these should not be revived.

The particular event which occasions this proposal occurred a few weeks ago. I was given some brandy. It was a brand which soon after was put on sale and pushed rather vigorously. It had a most elegant and convincing label, with five stars, a crest, French names and all—convincing, that is, till you noticed the absence of the name of a district in Cognac, or even of the word *Cognac*. I drank some—rather more than I would have wished, because the agents were so pressing. It had very little taste, but then so many things are characterless nowadays: they have all offensive characteristics removed, and all other characteristics too. It was smooth, as smooth as glycerin; but it had no bouquet. There was nothing positively wrong with it, that is; it only left a negative uneasiness.

That night, my heart began to beat with a sudden violence. I could feel it thumping between my ribs; my blood began to pulse so noisily that I could not sleep. My ears

throbbed. I sweated and my brain spun. I thought that I was suffering something unparalleled, until my mind rolled back over the last thirty years and I remembered.

You see, I lived and worked in New York in 1927 and 1928, *consule Coolidge*, as an editor of the *Encyclopædia Britannica*. Like any other visiting Englishman, I had my speakeasy tickets, and was fed bathtub gin by my hosts. Now I recalled what the results had been, and it was clear to me that once again I had been given hooch. Being a man with a civic conscience, I took it to a public analyst. From him I found that it did not contain the two best-known poisons of Prohibition days but was, as he said in very unbureaucratic language, "just a damned bad brandy." And since that was all that it was, there was nothing that he or I could do about it.

But I belong to a body that in centuries past was able to do some very drastic things about some "damned bad" commodities, and very possibly still theoretically could, since ancient statutes often lie about unrepealed. I would like to see its powers revived and imitated. It is French, one of the organizations that are generically called *confréries* of wine. You may have seen pictures of them at their festivals: the "Tastevins" of Burgundy wear silver saucers on silk ribbons round their necks, the "Baillis" of the Loire dress in black and yellow doublet-and-hose and look like medieval executioners, and the "Compagnons du Bontemps" in Médoc wear purple gowns and round hats that look like an imitation of a wooden bowl filled with white of egg (which is precisely what they are). Among these engaging societies, which are mostly modern publicity organizations, is one that is an ancient institution and that has survived, though with diminished powers, from the twelfth century. It is called the "Jurade," its home is the tiny town of St. Emilion (900 inhabitants) which makes a distinguished sort of claret, and it was founded in the reign of Richard Cœur de Lion, who was Duke of Aquitaine as well as King of England. It nearly faded out during the Victorian age, but not quite, for there is a continuous line of Premiers Jurats (the title of its chief) back to 1199, and since 1948 the Jurade has been very active again. As in all medieval bodies, its members occupy nicely distinguished ranks, and I have had the honor to be made a peer. On special occasions I have worn a long scarlet robe with a white hood, but usually I only wear a sort of scarf on my left shoulder, called an *épitoge*, in white silk with the arms of St. Emilion (leopards and fleurs-de-lis) on it in scarlet, blue, and gold.

When I was inducted, in an impressive ceremonial, I was informed of my duties, of which the main one was to expose and destroy any red wine that was of low quality and had been subjected to *fraude, frelaterie, magie, ou sorcellerie*. *Fraude* is a fairly easy word; *frelaterie* has the particular meaning of adding to a good wine (such as St. Emilion) a proportion of another wine rather like it; *magie* does differ from *sorcellerie* in some ways, but I am not sure how. *Magie* used to be the chief anxiety of the Jurade, but we have not been troubled much with it recently. Still, we take our precautions.

At vintage time, at rackings and at bottlings, all cellars, vats, *pressoirs*, and yards must be carefully cleared of all magical signs, curses, or cabalistic marks. The pentagram is held to be the most sinister design; it is described as "very powerful and exceptionally malignant." All women must be closely cross-questioned, and if found to be unclean or witches, removed from the parish. I have never yet been asked to take part in this; but I have been warned against bottling except under the waxing moon.

If, despite these precautions, a winegrower did make magicked, fraudulent, or adulterated wine, he used to be taken to a bleak, strong, square building on the hillside, still standing and called the Tour du Roi. There he was put in chains in a dungeon until the Jurade thought of him again. If there was no proof that the wine was magicked, fraudulent, or adulterated, but it was merely bad, the barrels were taken to the foot of the Tour du Roi and a great pile of furze and dried sticks built round them. Then they were fired, and as they burst and the alcohol burned off, there were some fine blue flames.

Another malpractice that the Jurade put down was that of making immature wine. The Jurats consulted with each other, watching the weather and testing the maturity of the grapes, until they decided on a date when harvesting could be commenced. This was called "proclaiming the ban," and it was done in much the same way as it is today. At the top of the Tour du Roi once again—for among all the charming buildings in St. Emilion the Jurade has always preferred this grim tower—stood the Premier Jurat with three colleagues, and behind them were trumpeters with silver trumpets. When they had made their announcement the trumpeters blew three notes and shouted, "Alleluia! St. Emilion!" The people waiting below answered, "Alleluia! St. Emilion!" and rushed off to their fields, not waiting to hear the final fanfare. But if any of them had started vintaging earlier, with green grapes, the Jurats went into their vineyards and simply poured the grape juice out on the ground.

In fairness to the Jurade it should be said that its functions were by no means only punishment. It offered protection against common dangers; for example, if I am attacked by archers, halberdiers, or bailiffs I can take refuge in any château in St. Emilion, and my wealth, life, and honor will be defended. I have sworn to offer the same assistance in North London to any Jurat who may need it. Moreover, good wine of which the Jurade approved was given its seal, which was branded on the cask.

The giving, or withholding, of the seal is about the only weapon the Jurade still wields. But the fact that its powers have been allowed to lapse does not prove that they were useless. They will have to be adapted to modern conditions. We cannot put in chains the producers of masses of indifferent and tasteless foods; it is no good going through their factories and stores looking for devilish signs to wipe out; we cannot even publicly burn what they make, or pour it out in the street. But penalties could be devised that would fit the crime.

Perhaps there is a useful precedent in the case of John Penroe, a seller of bad wine, whom the mayor and aldermen of London sentenced on November 11, 1350, to drink a copious draft of it, and have the rest poured over his head, "and to forswear the calling of vintner unless he can obtain the favour of our lord the King." Surely the directors and staff of the firm that produced that brandy of mine should be made to drink it. If they say it's good for the public, it's good for them. Just so, people who cross and hybridize trees until they get those large, highly colored fruits that look so well in the stores and have no taste whatever left in them, should be condemned to feed on nothing else.

But it's no good; one could speculate indefinitely upon just and satisfying punishment, but there is one

great flaw in the argument. The guilty would quite likely not feel that they were being punished at all. Tens of thousands of people are quite delighted to eat fruit that tastes of cotton wool, if it looks bright and is in a glossy package. They have never eaten a crisp, fresh, small nectarine, slightly spotted; they mightn't even like it. Even the hooch that I was sold—there are people who not only like it but are furious if deprived of it. The only remedy, I am afraid, is the slow one of pulling ourselves up by our own bootstraps. We must organize ourselves into societies in which each member is what the Germans call a *Feinschmecker* (finetaster).

It would be a presumption for me to think that I could educate fellow *Feinschmecker* in matters of taste generally. There is only one subject on which I think I dare say that I may be useful, and that is in the judging and tasting of wine. I have spent some years of thought and practice on it, and in addition I have had direct tuition, by precept and example, from my elders in the Jurade.

After I had been made a peer, I was allowed to attend, as a sort of pupil, an immense judging of the St. Emilion wines of 1949. There were between two and three hundred wines, as I recall, and 25 per cent of them were rejected. At each table of judging were four Jurats, four winegrowers, and four wine merchants. I watched carefully what they did, and from time to time they were kind enough to call me to taste a wine that was exceptionally good, or exceptionally bad, and would explain to me why. Nobody knew which any wine was, for in order to prevent any bias all labels had been washed off and numbers substituted. As the wine was at that date a young wine, the corks had been drawn ten hours before.

From this and from other experiences I have drawn up for myself a series of rules on how to get the best value out of wine—how to taste it in full, that is. If you will permit me, I shall now recite them, beginning from the moment of uncorking the bottle.

Firstly: Uncork the wine as early as you can. Letting the air into the wine starts a series of chemical changes, of which the first effect is to increase the flavor and the perfume. At the moment when the cork is drawn a wine is likely to be flat and dead. It may even have an unpleasant smell or taste. The first—the *very* first—smell of some of the finest and biggest Rhine wines is rather like Limburger cheese. You test that the next time you have one, if you doubt me. There is an odor of corruption which fortunately goes away very quickly. But if you are dining out, it is very difficult, in even the best restaurant, to get your wine uncorked

in good time. You can of course order it to be decanted, if you trust the restaurant so far. Or you may demand to see the wine list before you order any food, choose your wine, and have it sent for before you announce what you will eat. But that demands a good deal of obstinacy.

Secondly: Pour out a little of the wine into your glass and hold it up to the light, tipped at an angle of some 30 degrees. The object of this is firstly to admire its beauty and secondly to see if the wine is quite clear. If there are specks of dust or dirt in it, and even more if there is a trace of cloudiness, then you have been given a warning. Watch out for a dusty, muddy taste.

Thirdly: Swirl the wine round in the glass, hang your nose over the rim of it, and sniff. This, if you like technical terms, is called "taking the bouquet." It is a very important

part of the pleasure of wine tasting. (Of course, it is as well to have a large enough nose to do it with; the Father of his Country had a very fine nose for wine, and he used it too. When I visited Mount Vernon in an educational party in 1928, I saw some decanters at the back of a room, one of which at least had the word *Madeira* on it. "What did he use those jugs for?" I asked maliciously. "Grape juice," said our gray female escort savagely.) Every type of wine has its own perfume, and it is a delight to savor them all. I have often hunted for words to describe them, but I have never found any adequate. The smell of Rhine wines and Moselles is like a garden of spring flowers. The smell of sauternes is like the same garden later in the year. The full and almost dizzying smell of a big Burgundy reminds me of violets and blackberries. The smell of a splendid claret is the most elegant of all—it seems to have a series of scents in it, and it never has that suggestion of syrup which coarsens the others. The smell of Tokay is the most individual—it is *green*, like the smell of crushed grass and lush weeds trodden down in a meadow. And if the wine is not good, the smell will tell you that too. If it is a rooty, vinegary, or musty wine, it will have a rooty, vinegary, or musty smell, and your nose will save you the unpleasant experience of drinking it.

Fourthly: Now I will allow you to take a mouthful of the wine. But do not gulp it. Roll it round your mouth, and hold it there long enough to breathe in and out once

ILLUSTRATED FOR HORIZON BY GERRY GERSTEN

through the nose. As you do that, you will notice that the taste changes. A mouthful of boiled egg is a mouthful of boiled egg; not so a glass of wine. It continues to develop until the last moment, which is—

Fifthly—when you swallow it. For as it goes down, pleasantly washing your tonsils, a good wine leaves a farewell faint flavor which there is no reason to waste.

By now, I have no doubt, you are protesting that all this is unnecessary. May not a man take a glass of wine without all this fuss? Certainly he may; and not even I would go through all this ceremonial except for the first glass that comes out of a bottle. But I am an obstinately economical man, and I know that for the first glass it is good sense and good business. I have paid for four different sorts of sensations in my wine; why shouldn't I have them? Without doubt, it involves taking trouble, of a sort. But what sort of trouble? Merely the trouble of noticing. And that is the essence of pleasure. All pleasures have to be noticed. An unnoticed pleasure is not a pleasure at all. The idea of it is a contradiction in terms.

But there is a sound instinct behind the protest that I have assumed you are making. A large number of writers gain an honest living, or at any rate a living, by pontifical books and articles on wine drinking that make it sound a difficult art, which only they and their refined friends can practice. It is everybody's duty to object if more obstacles are added to those which have already been piled up. But so far from wishing to do that, I shall now proceed to knock away a good deal of the pile.

These people are properly called Wine Snobs, and I would have liked to deal with them gently. Not only are any snobs fascinating to watch, but as these drink wine and often know quite a lot about it, there must be a foundation of civilization in them. But what a complicated, machicolated fortress of conceit they have built on that foundation! There are more of them, I think, in Britain than in America; they proliferate in the wealthier suburbs, especially at bridge

parties and tennis parties, and they infest certain West End clubs. They are nearly all male—a female Wine Snob is rare (though very dangerous when found)—they are of all ages, and their chief object is to convict someone else of ignorance or of an error in taste. To make this easy for them, they have constructed a twisted mass of precepts and rules that are partly pointless and partly untrue. To trip them, put them down, expose them, and prove them wrong is not only a pleasure but a moral duty, for conversational bullies are a nuisance and spiritual pride is a sin.

Here follows, then, a résumé of the chief gambits that they use to impose their authority, and an exposition of the way of countering them and proving them wrong.

The commonest of all, of course, is to talk about vintages. The supersnob pretends to carry all vintage years since 1906 in his head; the second-grade has a little card in his pocket, ruled in squares, in which seven types of wine are classified from 0 to 7. When one of them says, "1948? Oh, yes, I suppose so. But a rather poor year, don't you think?" the average diner trembles. But he need not. For the fact is that these cards are delusive, and this talk about vintages (except strictly professional talk in wine merchants' offices) is mostly nonsense. Vineyards vary enormously, according to their site. One will have just that much more sun, less rain, or stronger wind than the next in a given year, and in every "good" year there are many vineyards which have produced poor wine, and in every "bad" year almost as many which have produced good wine. The fact is, if a winegrower puts the date of a year—any year—on his bottle, then he thinks it was a good year for him, and he is likely to know. If you would like to record for your own pleasure those years which he is most likely to put on his bottles, here they are: 1945, 1947, 1948, 1949, 1950, 1952, 1953, 1955. These figures are valid for all European wines, except that I would not buy anything more than ten years old, bar French red wines.

Their next most successful line of attack is to suggest that you have served a wine in the wrong glass. Certainly, there are in glassware stores pretty things called sherry glasses, brandy glasses, Rhine wine glasses, and Burgundy glasses. But they are table ornaments, nothing else. The Wine Snob is the victim of his own imaginings if he thinks they have any vinous reason to exist, or that it is "correct" to use them. You need have only one glass. There is one glass, of the traditional shape, and one only, which will serve better than any other for every wine, and every spirit too; its qualities can be deduced from the five principles set out above. It is colorless, so that you can see the wine clearly. It is reason-

CONTINUED ON PAGE 145

107

BOLTON LANDING *by Willem de Kooning*

108

People's Choice

Three new works by painters in demand

tell of the far-ranging diversity

of American art and of the rival tastes of its patrons

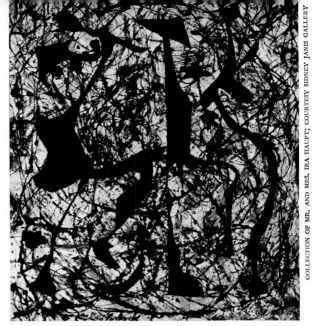

SHADOWED *by Jackson Pollock*

Willem de Kooning's *Bolton Landing*, opposite, is a new work by one of the most discussed and sought-after painters in America today. With its explosive violence it has little in common with the paintings shown in color on the pages that follow: Jack Levine's *Inauguration* and Andrew Wyeth's *Roasted Chestnuts*. Yet these, too, are very recent works by outstanding Americans. Together the contrasting pictures exemplify the range of inspiration as well as of acceptance of American art at this moment.

The three were completed within little more than a year of one another, De Kooning's and Levine's in New York City and Wyeth's in his rural home at Chadds Ford in southeastern Pennsylvania. Each one represents a major school or movement in which its painter is a leading figure. De Kooning's school, the newest and currently the most publicized, is the radical Abstract Expressionist wing of the revolt against representation of "real" things. And he adheres to the most radical wing of *that* wing, namely the group who believe in spontaneously throwing their impulses upon canvas and who are called "action" painters.

Levine and Wyeth, on the other hand, are obviously "realists"—although that word can mean many things. Levine, with his interpretive analysis of modern life and institutions, works in a vein sometimes called "social realism," while Wyeth stems from an older tradition of meticulous, thoughtful representation that has been termed "literalism" by those who don't like it and, in his adaptation of it, "magic realism" by many who do. But these labels do not necessarily satisfy: upon looking first at these pictures one might also say that De Kooning is evidently highly subjec-

tive and emotional in his approach, Levine critical and humanistic, and Wyeth reflective and poetic. In any case, what is more significant than the labels is the fact that three such contrasting schools of painting should exist side by side in America today, all enjoying large followings among divergent patrons.

In terms of the market place, De Kooning (now in his middle fifties) and Levine and Wyeth (in their early forties) are all top performers. Although current fashion leans to the abstractionists, the prices commanded for major works by Wyeth and Levine are higher than those fetched by De Kooning and run into five figures. The production rate of such works by all three, moreover, is slow: Wyeth completes only two or three of his painstaking temperas per year, while Levine spent upwards of eighteen months off-and-on on *Inauguration*, and De Kooning, for all his air of improvisation, delivered only one painting in all of 1957— *Bolton Landing*. All three are sought after by museums that seek to embrace the range of outstanding twentieth-century American art—and no curator is any surer than is any private collector of what will "last."

Coming from the painters' scarcity production and amid such catholicity of taste, these three recent works were all snapped up at once. The range of their buyers again shows up the diversity of interest in current art. Wyeth's *Roasted Chestnuts* was bought by a private collector, Republican Congressman Harry G. Haskell, Jr., of Delaware, a friend and neighbor of the painter. Levine's *Inauguration* was acquired by the Sara M. Roby Foundation, a fund set up by Mrs. Roby of New York, herself a painter, for the purchase of notable new indigenous work. The Foundation is now building a collection with the advice of New York's Whitney Museum of American Art, which houses its purchases and makes them available for loans.

Meanwhile, the third and certainly most controversial of the three paintings, De Kooning's, was taken by another type of collector now also influencing the art world—a corporation with money to spend on decorating its offices. The days are long past when large business organizations felt their debt to art was done by commissioning a portrait of the founder, usually in dark, academic oils, for reverential hanging in the Board Room. Today, a collector's spirit has been unloosed in many businesses either by an art-loving top executive, or by impulses of prestige, or in some cases by architects whose designs call for modern art to accompany a modern building. Over the years, companies ranging from the International Business Machines Corporation to the Abbott Laboratories at Chicago have been steadily buying American works of many schools. On New York's Park Avenue, the spectacular new office building designed by Mies van der Rohe and Philip Johnson for Seagram Distillers houses paintings of such abstractionists as Adolph Gottlieb, Mark Rothko, and Philip Guston. The purchaser of *Bolton Landing* is the Inland Steel Company, whose executives may also ponder abstract sculptures set up in their new Chicago headquarters building when they are not absorbed in the manufacture of rails, bars, sheets, and blooms.

To conservative holdovers at Inland Steel who may be asking what *Bolton Landing* really means, the answer is that it is not intended to resemble Bolton's or any other landing. The painter was not painting an object but his own state of mind. Born in Rotterdam in 1904, De Kooning came to this country in the 1920's as a young painter influenced by his fellow countrymen, the turbulent Vincent van Gogh and the early, calm abstractionist Piet Mondrian. Eventually turbulence won out: De Kooning became not only an all-out abstractionist but one of the extreme group determined to put on canvas their immediate emotional responses without any reference to preconceived design. Of this "action" school, with its reliance on impulse and the unconscious, Jackson Pollock was the most famous prophet. Some of its members do not title their canvases but simply number them (in Pollock's case, after having spread them on the floor and walked over them while dripping paint on them). In the case of *Bolton Landing*, the title is derived only from the fact that De Kooning paid a visit to his friend and fellow abstractionist, sculptor David Smith, at a place on Lake George called Bolton Landing, after which he was inspired to paint.

While De Kooning's work arouses reactions that range from intense admiration to outright rage, most critics credit him with great sincerity and earnestness of purpose. For the sheer violence he transmits to canvas, he knows no peer. "Art

never seems to me peaceful or pure," he has said, adding that "nothing is positive about art, except that it is a word."

Jack Levine's *Inauguration*, on the other hand, obviously does represent an inauguration—although none that a viewer can actually identify. It might be said to represent the general spirit and mood of American political life at a typical ceremonial moment, as a clinical observer sees it. Levine, born in South Boston in 1915, was raised with early memories of slum life and then was swept up in the wave of social protest that marked the 1930's. As an aspiring painter he was first influenced by the modern Frenchmen Soutine and Rouault. As a critic, Levine turned to satire and sermon.

His present painting is one of a series of commentaries cast in the same size, in which he has looked successively at the underworld (*Gangster Funeral*), the courts (*The Trial*), the world of professional politicians (*Election Night*), and old-time show business (*Medicine Show*). "I've done the judiciary and the executive branches, and I suppose I'll do the legislative," he remarks—and with *Inauguration* out of the way, he is thinking about just that.

Inauguration was begun in October, 1956, and although photographs of President Eisenhower's second installation were used as research for it, the chief figures are obviously of Levine's own imagining, while their dress could place them anywhere over the last fifty years. As for the presidential figure in his painting, he now thinks it rather resembles Woodrow Wilson, although he had no one specifically in mind when he set out. He sees his oath taker as a respectable, honest person, but lacking in human warmth—"a man I could never warm up to." There is detailed characterization in the work but, Levine says, no caricature. "I wasn't trying to be fresh," he remarks, "I wanted to make a comment on the political situation. I think the lighting sets the mood."

In his critical approach and his concern with the ways of human society, Levine stems from a broad tradition that first flowered in this country with the so-called Ashcan School of American realists soon after the turn of the century. In the 1930's, a second generation that brought forth new lights such as Ben Shahn and Philip Evergood added political fervor and sometimes even revolutionary dynamite to the mixture—as well as a sharper, harsher, more personal style of painting. Today a mellowed Ben Shahn at sixty has long since ceased drawing under the sign of the Left, and in the course of making his peace with the world he has also become one of the most popular of American painters. The less-renowned Evergood, too, has turned from social tragedy to the human comedy. But their old astringency of observation is still there, as it is also in the younger Levine.

With Andrew Wyeth we come to an even older tradition, and one that many insurgents have pronounced dead. Born in 1917, the son of the illustrator N. C. Wyeth, he was trained by his father in the craft of meticulous repre-

INAUGURATION *by Jack Levine*

111

THRESHOLD TO SUCCESS *by Philip Evergood*

STED CHESTNUTS *by Andrew Wyeth*

sentation that had made the Wyeth name famous. But something more went into the home-grown young student than just that. Before his father's time, American painters like Thomas Eakins and Winslow Homer had painted from nature in a way that combines precision with depth of portrayal and a sense of brooding atmosphere. Much of this somber poetry reappears in the work of the second Wyeth, who paints homely and familiar scenes in which his neighbors at Chadds Ford and in summertime Maine are often the actors, but whose undertones bring intimations of wider meanings.

Roasted Chestnuts, the artist explains, was inspired by his seeing a neighborhood youth standing in the winter cold hoping to sell chestnuts to some passing motorist. Wyeth was struck by the way the December sunlight touched the back of the boy's head, by his lean tallness in his army jacket, by the color of the Osage orange hedge behind him, and by the quiet of a scene marked chiefly by the steam rising from the boy's homemade chestnut roaster. Tire marks in the roadway showed that some car, not too long before, had come and gone. Wyeth felt that this setting was symbolic of loneliness as well as expectancy, and so he set out to paint it.

Beginning with a simple subject, then, what finally emerges is an image of subtle, far-reaching poignancy. In a comparable way, Wyeth's senior in the realist tradition, Edward Hopper, has been able over the years to invest such matter-of-fact objects as a line of brownstone house fronts or an all-night beanery or a bare room by the sea with a lyric quality of his own. "My aim in painting," Hopper has said, "has always been the most exact transmission

possible of my most intimate impressions of nature." This appears to be Wyeth's intent, too, and the result of such realism has led many to preface it with the adjective *magic*.

Of the various approaches and attitudes that De Kooning, Levine, and Wyeth typify, which is the one of the greatest relevance today or that points the way to the future? The subject is, of course, being hotly debated. In selecting an exhibit of "New American Painting" to be shown in many European cities in 1958–1959, the International Council of the Museum of Modern Art picked only works of abstractionists. Yet at the same time dealers report that demand for artists of precisely the opposite persuasion, such as Wyeth, Levine, Shahn, Hopper, and Charles Burchfield, is at a steady high. The Solomon R. Guggenheim Museum in New York buys almost nothing but nonrepresentational art; on the other hand, the foundation endowed by another member of the same family in memory of John Simon Guggenheim enthusiastically gives grants to artists who do represent as well as to those who don't. The Museum of Fine Arts at Dallas, Texas, reports that it would like to have a painting by the abstractionist Mark Tobey, but that it would like one by Wyeth, too. By contrast, the Art Museum at Wichita, Kansas, disposing of the extensive Roland P. Murdock endowment for buying American art, still will not have any of the new Abstract Expressionists in the house. Art students at the nearby University of Wichita, though, are reported to be abstractionists almost to a man.

In many other times and places, one accepted or even "official" style was preferred against all others, to the point of excluding them. Conversely, in the time of the then radical Impressionists and their insurgent successors in France, *they* soon became accepted as the painters to be prized by all persons of taste, while conservatives and academicians were laughed at. But in America today we find a busy and tense coexistence of many styles each hoping to outdo the other, which may mean either that our tastes are very broad or that they are somewhat unstable.

Is this possibly a transitional period in art that must lead to some resolution? Will something of the American realist tradition eventually shine forth through the experiments of those who have broken from it? There are indications that at least a few abstractionists are turning back to an interest in nature. One of them, young Richard Diebenkorn of California, has also returned to painting the human figure, keeping alive his love of spontaneity but at the same time revealing the influence of the rigorous Edward Hopper. On the other hand, will the abstractionists' discoveries in sheer surface texture and excitement influence the realists? No two observers yet appear able to agree on a Trend. In the meantime, we have among us so many corporations with a surplus, so many wealthy individuals who can earn a tax cut by endowing a collection, and so many smaller buyers keen on taking a chance, that the vigorous battle of the paintings is being encouraged to go on.

FOUR LANE ROAD *by Edward Hopper*

113

After generations of trial and error, man's age-old dream of flying was realized near the end of the eighteenth century in the form—or rather forms—shown here. Throughout several decades, daring aeronauts gave play to their imaginations by constructing ever more fanciful balloons and performing increasingly startling feats before gaping audiences. Finally in 1855 ballooning enthusiasts were treated to this Paris-published panorama entitled *Ascensions Aerostatiques Les Plus Remarquables*, recalling great flights undertaken in pursuit of "the art of aerostation . . . the most audacious conception of human genius." No. 1 (lower left) shows a pioneer effort that never got off the ground: Jesuit Father Lana's scheme in 1670 to lift a "flying boat" with lighter-than-air vacuum globes. Nos. 2 and 3: Montgolfier's first hot-air, unmanned balloons. No. 5: the first living creatures to be carried experimentally aloft, 1783—a sheep, a rooster, and a duck. No. 7: man's first free ascent, later the same year—Pilâtre de Rozier and the Marquis d'Arlandes taking off from Paris. No. 14: an early, unsuccessful effort to steer a balloon by wings. No. 20: Mazet's and Bremont's balloon burns up, Marseilles, 1784. No. 29: Don J. Patinho ascends in Spain, in "an aerostat in the form of a fish with oars and rudder." No. 36: De Rozier and Romain meet disaster while crossing the Channel. No. 44: equestrian ascension, 1798 (later improved on by the ascension of a horse and carriage with passengers, No. 74). Nos. 47-48 (top): Gay-Lussac reaches a record height of 23,000 feet. No. 50: Aeronaut Mosment has the "unbelievable temerity" to ascend on a platform (on which he lost his balance and fell off). No. 57: Robertson descends from his balloon by parachute, Lisbon, 1819. No. 66: new attempt at steering by means of paddles, reportedly conducted by a Mr. Taggett at Lowell, Massachusetts, 1850. No. 71: model dirigible tested "with some success" at the Paris Hippodrome, also in 1850. Nos. 78 and 79: fantastic proposals for airships. No. 80: one of the briefest and oddest flights of all: "Mlle. Juannita Perez raises herself up and floats in the air above the promenade of the Prado, Madrid, using a mechanism of wings invented by her father, Don Diego de Salamanca."

WHEN
MAN
FIRST
LEFT
THE
ARTH

47 et 48

65

57

*For the
Great Age of Ballooning
turn the page*

51

73

34

62

38

45

54

23

64

35

39

41

50

66

70

58

9

40

36

5

56

67

61

30

43

74

60

68

44

52

71

42

76

49

75

81

53

37

69

WHEN MAN FIRST LEFT THE EARTH

Festive crowds cheered

and sages applauded

when daring aeronauts

opened the ballooning era

in an atmosphere of

wonder and exuberance

By PETER LYON

On a November afternoon in 1783, two spirited young Frenchmen departed this planet from the Bois de Boulogne, soared up over the Seine, sailed past the Invalides, and after a journey lasting twenty-five minutes settled safely to earth again on the far side of Paris. Their feat was unprecedented: it ushered in the age of space travel. Since it was, moreover, the culmination of a creative effort that had enlisted the minds of philosophers, poets, and scientists for a thousand years, and the realization of a dream that had captured man's imagination since first he envied the flight of a bird, the feat was everywhere joyously hailed with a gay and spontaneous enthusiasm. Hundreds of thousands of people had witnessed the marvel: some wept in an agony of apprehension while the two aeronauts yet floated in their balloon; some fell to their knees in prayer; all, as the balloon glided grandly to its landing, cheered themselves hoarse. The American envoy, Benjamin Franklin, was there. Later someone asked him of what use was a balloon. "Of what use," Franklin retorted, "is a new-born baby?"

This epochal flight was consummated by the simplest of devices. Massive intellects—Roger Bacon, Leonardo da Vinci, Emanuel Swedenborg—had all considered the problem of flight, but all had foundered on the ornithopter principle; that is to say, all had peered at the birds and in consequence had stubbornly insisted on contraptions with flapping wings. Over the centuries, dozens of men endowed with more pluck than logic had plunged to their death, martyrs to that principle. Even those who deprecated the notion of flight, like the essayist Joseph Addison, protested because, they argued, the skill would entail a bird brain and, as well, the alleged promiscuity of a bird. "It would fill the world with innumerable immoralities," Addison wrote. "The cupola of St. Paul's [would be] covered with both sexes like the outside of a pigeon-house." But the man who made possible the first human aerial journey was not concerned with the birds. He sent his aeronauts up under 2,200 cubic meters of hot air.

The balloon's inventor was Joseph Montgolfier, elder son of a paper manufacturer of Annonay, near Lyon. Both Joseph and his brother Etienne had grappled for some time with the mystery of flying. They were familiar with Joseph Priestley's *Experiments and Observations on Different Kinds of Air*, and Joseph had tinkered with parachutes, successfully dropping a sheep from a tower under a rig designed like a parasol. One day in 1782 Joseph was lounging in a chimney corner in Avignon, staring at an engraving that showed the French and Spanish besieging the British at Gibraltar. The allies, as he knew, had been blocked: neither by land nor by sea could they hack their way onto the Rock. But, he asked himself, why not by air? Smoke rises in the air, he thought, staring now at the fire on the hearth beside him. Couldn't enough smoke be stored somehow to lift a man?

Countless generations of men had noticed that smoke rises. But it was not until the age of reason that this observation would be seized upon by a man who knew the weight, porosity, and tensile strength of silk and paper, and who had, moreover, an inquiring mind and a lively imagination; a man who, in the phrase of a contemporary, would think to "enclose a cloud in a bag."

On the spur of his idea, Montgolfier sprang up, found some scraps of taffeta, and at once contrived a small spherical bag. Gently he cradled its open end over a flame for a moment, and then—wide-eyed and wondering—he watched as it floated up to the ceiling. "Get some taffeta and ropes ready," he wrote his brother Etienne, "and you will see the most amazing sights in the world."

The brothers were ready for their first public demonstration at Annonay by June, 1783. When their linen-and-paper balloon was filled with hot air it rose gracefully into a rainy sky and stayed aloft in free, unmarred flight for ten minutes. At once the success was reported to the Academy in Paris, where it filled the savants with excitement. The brothers were invited north to repeat their experiment; but by the time of their arrival, one of the academicians, the eminent physicist, Professor J. A. C. Charles, had designed his own balloon of a different type. The report from Annonay suggested that the Montgolfiers had used a gas of their own invention (actually they had used only straw and wool to feed their fire). Professor Charles, however, thought that hydrogen, the recent discovery of Henry Cavendish, should prove adequate. Unlike the open-necked Montgolfière, the first Charlière was closed by a valve to contain the gas. Word of Charles's strange undertaking swept over the city: when the balloon was transported by night through the streets to the Champ de Mars, the people bared their heads and knelt in wonder as it went by under armed guard. Next afternoon cannon boomed, heralding the ascension, and all Paris exulted. The balloon rose into a sunny sky and soared away, north and east, out of sight. Somewhere aloft, the expanding hydrogen tore a rent in the taffeta. It floated down in farm country, scaring the peasants out of their wits. They summoned the parish priest to exorcise the "writhing demon from the clouds" with bell, book, and candle; when this recipe was unavailing, they dispatched it with scythe, flail, and blunderbuss.

By now Etienne Montgolfier had arrived in Paris (Joseph was deemed a trifle uncouth for court society) and had set about the construction of his *globe volant*. Aware that he was among the quality, Etienne created a magnificent blue aerostat seventy-four feet high, girdled it with scarlet swags, and decorated it with zodiacal signs, wreaths, portraits of Apollo, and royal ciphers, all in gold. The handsome creation was tested in free flight with three passengers—a sheep, a cock, and a duck—suspended in a wicker basket under the balloon's open neck. All three having weathered their trip satisfactorily, thought was now given to the concept of human freight. There were volunteers aplenty, some of them quite clamorous; but word came from His August Majesty, Louis XVI, that no human life was to be imperiled by such fool nonsense except it be that of a convict. Here was a gage flung down before every Frenchman of spirit. It was intolerable. Happily, it was also rescinded, and the volunteers could be heeded.

Of these, the most importunate was a physician named François Pilâtre de Rozier, who in October was lifted in captive flight first to 84 feet, then four days later to 210 feet, still later to 262 feet, and at length to 330 feet. All these trials with the balloon at anchor having proved that the air up there was not poisonous, on November 21 the balloon was again inflated, Pilâtre was joined on the gallery by the Marquis d'Arlandes, a brazier was slung in the neck of the balloon (to be stoked or damped down, as required, through portholes), lines were cast off, and Man was launched on his first trip into space. An account by d'Arlandes is at hand:

"I was astonished at the silence . . . that our departure occasioned among the spectators; I thought perhaps, dumfounded and even terrified by the novel spectacle, they needed reassurance. I waved my handkerchief and presently I saw great excitement below. At this moment, M. Pilâtre called: 'You do nothing and we shall not mount.' 'Pardon me,' I answered, 'but it was very necessary to reassure those unhappy humans whom we leave below in a plight less pleasant than ours.' I put some straw on the fire. . . .

"I said to my brave companion: 'There's a river which is very hard to cross.' 'I well believe it,' he answered, 'for you are doing nothing.' I pitched some straw into the fire . . . I now saw some holes [burned in the balloon] of which some were quite large. I said then: 'We must descend.' 'Why?' 'Look . . .'

"I took my sponge and easily extinguished the bit of fire that licked at those holes I could reach; but, having perceived . . . that the cloth [of the balloon] was coming apart very easily, I repeated to my brave companion, 'We must descend.' He looked beneath him and said: 'We are over Paris.' 'No matter,' I told him; 'but . . . are you all right?' 'Yes.' I examined again on my side and saw that there was nothing to fear . . . So I said: 'We can cross Paris . . .'

"We damped down the fire; the intrepid Pilâtre . . . called out, 'Watch out for the windmills!' But . . . I saw that we could not hit them, and I told him: 'We are landing!'"

They landed; and in the process the intrepid Pilâtre's redingote was torn to bits by the crowd for souvenirs, so that only d'Arlandes was in a position to appear before the Academy to report on the historic trip.

Ten days later the rival Professor Charles, having slung a "car" under the first big hydrogen balloon, soared up from the Tuileries together with an assistant and sailed away to the northwest. It was a lovely, limpid day; Charles reported that as they drifted along he could hear men below shouting to them:

"My good friends, have you no fear? Are you not sick at all? O God, how beautiful it is! We pray that God may keep you; adieu, my friends!"

The two men landed at Nesle, twenty-seven miles away; but Charles promptly took off again alone, rising to 9,000 feet, where, in solitary wonder, he watched the sun set for the second time in the same day.

Here then, all at once, mankind found itself with two splendid new toys. They were simplicity itself to make; they were reasonably safe to operate; they were a joy to behold not only for their vivid gores and gay adornments but for their round, plump shape; even more, they were exhilarating to ride in. Was it any wonder that overnight an aerostatic craze was touched off?

"You will observe, Madam," wrote Dr. Johnson to Mrs. Thrale, "that the balloon engages all mankind." It was no less than the truth: the balloon was a godsend to people with all sorts of notions—to statesmen, pondering power; to lovers, plotting elopements; to rascals, scheming of great smuggling coups; to romancers, puzzling how to extricate their heroes from desperate dilemmas; to political cartoonists, blissful as they contemplated the possibilities offered by gas and hot air; but most of all to designers and craftsmen. From the ateliers of these folk poured a bewildering profusion of items—glazed pottery from Delft, exquisite porcelain from Sèvres, faïence from Moustiers and Marseille; mirrors and clocks, chair backs and bird cages, snuffboxes and fans, even elegant *pot-pots*—all with a balloon motif, usually commemorative of some celebrated flight. The *couturiers* and hairdressers jostled their way into the act too, with the customary outrageous results.

In all the ferment of joyous activity, only the soldiers stood glumly apart. They failed to see how the balloon would appreciably assist them in their task of killing larger numbers of people. The same consideration, but from a different angle of vision, had already occurred to Horace Walpole. "I hope," wrote that tireless correspondent, "that these new mechanic meteors will prove only playthings for the learned and the idle, and not be converted into new engines of destruction to the human race, as is so often the case of refine-

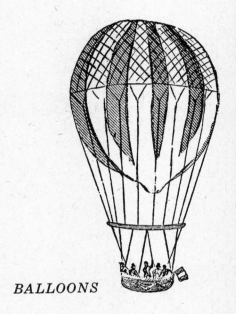

BALLOONS

Journeying on high, the silken castle glides,
Bright as a meteor through the azure tides,
O'er towns, and towers, and temples wins its way,
Or mounts sublime, and gilds the vault of day.
Silent, with upturned eyes, unbreathing crowds
Pursue the floating wonder to the clouds,
And, flushed with transport, or benumbed with fear,
Watch, as it rises, the diminished sphere.
—Now less and less—and now a speck is seen;
And now the fleeting rack obtrudes between . . .
The calm philosopher in ether sails,
Views broader stars, and breathes in purer gales,
Sees, like a map, in many a waving line,
Round Earth's blue plains her lucid waters shine;
Sees at his feet the forky lightnings glow,
And hears innocuous thunders roar below.

ERASMUS DARWIN,
The Loves of the Plants, 1789

ments or discoveries in science." Benjamin Franklin was at once alarmed and hopeful. "Convincing Sovereigns of the Folly of Wars, may perhaps be one Effect of [the discovery]," he wrote to a friend in Vienna. For "Where is the Prince who can afford to so cover his Country with Troops for its Defense, as that Ten Thousand Men descending from the Clouds, might not in many Places do an infinite deal of Mischief, before a Force could be brought together to repel them?" But to the military the doleful fact was that the direction of a balloon could not be controlled, save up or down. Otherwise it was at the mercy of the wind; and, on those terms, What price destruction?

This limitation of movement vexed some of the aeronauts too. It was not enough to rise and soar and see below them a vast countryside unfolding like a map; being human and therefore contrary, they yearned when the wind was this way to go that. Of these, the most persistent was Jean-Pierre Blanchard, a small, stubborn, disagreeable man who nevertheless did more than any other to popularize aerostation. In a sense he did it reluctantly, for he was committed to heavier-than-air flight. Between 1781 and 1783 he had designed a *vaisseau volant* on the ornithopter principle; it was almost completely hidden under a cloudbank of rudders, sails, propellers, fins, and even great winged oars. All this paraphernalia he now attached to a parachute under a balloon and gravely set about attempting to row through the air. More important, as a professional aeronaut he attracted great crowds to one launching after another, which he conducted under a slogan taken from Vergil, *Sic itur ad astra* (This way the road to the stars), and to which he charged a stiff admission fee.

His demonstrations, almost without exception, were animated by displays of Gallic temperament. At his first, at the Champ de Mars in March, 1784, a military cadet (later erroneously identified as Napoleon Bonaparte) tried at the moment of take-off to force his way aboard. Foiled, he drew his sword, pinked Blanchard on the chest, broke the oars, and tore the parachute. The exasperated Blanchard sailed away for an hour or so, returning only to find that in his absence some unfriendly wit had created an epigram:

> *Au Champ de Mars il s'envola*
> *Au champ voisin; il resta là.*
> *Beaucoup d'argent il ramassa,*
> *Messieurs,* Sic itur ad astra.

Soon the balloon was causing more trouble on land. By April, 1784, unscheduled landings of Montgolfières large and small had started so many fires in the fields and had in consequence so incensed the peasantry that the French government issued an ordinance—the first affecting air travel—forbidding unauthorized ascensions; soon the emperor of Austria, the king of Spain, and a clutch of German princes were all obliged to announce similar laws. By May the balloon had caused its first *bagarre* at Bordeaux. The *bagarre* is a characteristically French uproar, obscure of origin, murky, violent, and passionate. On this occasion, a balloon could not be inflated, and before the tumult had been quelled, two men had been shot, two more hanged, and nine condemned to the galleys.

Happily, the ascensions were not always so boisterous. At Lyon in June, a Montgolfière called *La Gustave* in honor of King Gustav III of Sweden, who was present somewhat incognito, rose with the first woman passenger in history, a Mme Thible. In a transport, the lady warbled snatches of song from Grétry's comic opera *Zémire et Azor:* "Je triomphe," she caroled, "je suis reine!" And, sure enough, that night she was crowned at the Comédie.

But in the face of all this, what of the English? The French, smoothing down their back hair with some condescension, had it that the English were sulking, mortified at the threat posed to their maritime supremacy by this new aerial navigation. And it is true that the first flight in England was made by an Italian, Vincent Lunardi, a dashing secretary in the Neapolitan Embassy at London. On September 15, 1784, Lunardi floated up from the Artillery Ground before a huge and—so the French insisted—skeptical throng. He had with him a pigeon, a cat, and a dog. The pigeon flew off, the cat jumped out of the basket when Lunardi touched down for a moment at North Mimms, but the dog stayed with him to the last, twenty-four miles in a little over two hours. The Italian woke next day to find himself a hero; he was lionized by the London ladies; Lunardi bonnets, even Lunardi garters were the rage. Not all, however, were his admirers. "I was very angry with him, wrote Horace Walpole, "he had full right to venture his own neck, but none to risk the poor cat." Dr. Johnson, too, was grumpy. "The vehicles can serve no use till we can guide them," he wrote; "I had rather now find a medicine that can ease an asthma."

The brave balloonists were undaunted by such evidence of disfavor. There were still hurdles to leap, still "firsts" to establish. The first to make an ascension in Ireland was Sir Richard Crosbie, who seemed determined at least to set the mark for sartorial splendor. His "aerial costume consisted of a robe of oiled silk lined with white fur, his waistcoat and breeches in one of white satin quilted, and morocco boots and a Montero cap of leopard skin." The first English woman to climb into the air was Mrs. Letitia Ann Sage, a beauty of generous proportions (she weighed in at 200 pounds) who was to have gone up with Lunardi and a friend, George Biggin. At the last moment, however, Lunardi was obliged

o step aside, for the balloon would lift only two. Biggin and Mrs. Sage came down in a field near Harrow, where they were set upon by an indignant rustic; the schoolboys of Harrow gallantly rescued her.

But the most challenging hurdle was the English Channel. To cross it was the pet project of Jean-Pierre Blanchard, and he found an angel in an American physician, Dr. John Jeffries. Since he had paid all Blanchard's expenses, Dr. Jeffries naturally assumed he was to go on the flight; but Blanchard wanted the glory alone and even went so far as to weight himself down with lead in his effort to persuade Jeffries that the balloon would not lift them both. After an appeal to the governor of Dover Castle, the lead was removed from Blanchard's pants, Jeffries was admitted to the basket, and off they sailed under a leaky balloon, encumbered with Blanchard's customary quota of futile propellers, oars, and rudders. The crossing itself was nip and tuck. All their ballast was gone before they were halfway over; gradually they jettisoned everything else they could: flags, anchors, brandy, oars and rudder, even—despite the chill January weather—their coats. Just off the coast of Calais, Blanchard shucked off his trousers as well and tossed them into the drink. Luckily the aeronauts found an updraft that took them inland, but then they faced the danger of crashing in a forest. At this point, the doctor bethought himself of one last resort for lightening ship and proposed that both relieve their bladders. This, he later reported, "I have reason to believe was of *real utility* to us, in our then situation." They were safe but nearly frozen when they finally came down some twelve miles inland from Calais.

Once again, here was a genuine achievement and a feat to capture the popular imagination. Honors were heaped on both men; the flight touched off another spate of speculations about cross-Channel invasions; but on a more prosaic level it summoned up only reflections on the delays the traveler of the future might be spared. "If there is no airsickness," said Horace Walpole decisively, "and I were to go to Paris again, I would prefer a balloon to the packet-boat." Then as now, to most Englishmen Paris connoted naughty weekend excursions. And so a verse went the rounds of London:

> Ye masters of Packets! Ye poor silly loons!
> Sell your boats and get Blanchard to make you balloons;
> For our fair modern Witches, no longer aquatic,
> Will never more cross but in boats Aerostatic.

The jubilation over this heroic venture was somewhat sobered by the ill-starred attempt to duplicate it from the opposite direction. For political reasons, a French minister goaded Pilâtre de Rozier into the effort, insisting on the flight even against Pilâtre's more prudent judgment. And so the world's first aeronaut became as well the world's first air casualty. Pilâtre had hoped to avert the risks of the Blanchard-Jeffries trip by combining into one craft the principles of both the Montgolfière and the Charlière. The result, a spherical hydrogen envelope surmounting a hot-air cylinder, was called a Rozière. But it was the only one ever built. The hydrogen caught fire; Pilâtre and a companion, in a spectacular crash, tumbled to their death on the French coast.

But not this tragedy, nor even such a titanic political upheaval as the French Revolution, could take all the gilt off the gingerbread. For by now the professionals, dedicated and single-minded like all true birdmen, were wholly involved; they were disposed to let revolutions run their course; regardless, they would soar on. Lunardi, seduced from diplomacy by the pleasures of flight and the even headier pleasures of extravagant adulation, toured the British Isles and later Spain and Portugal. Blanchard established "firsts" all over the map: in Germany at Frankfurt, in Holland at The Hague, in Belgium at Ghent, in Switzerland at Basel, in Poland at Warsaw, in Bohemia at Prague, and finally in 1793 a hemispheric "first" in the United States at Philadelphia.

There had been a few abortive attempts in America to lift a passenger by balloon before Blanchard's arrival, but his was officially regarded as the maiden flight. Since Philadelphia was then the capital of the infant country, the affair was conducted with full official pomp: President Washington was there to hand Blanchard a passport that he might show to any citizen moved to offer him hindrance or molestation; most of the Cabinet was there; so was the French minister plenipotentiary, and so were many congressmen.

Although he was still stubbornly convinced that "at any height in the atmosphere" he "might direct [the balloon's] motions at pleasure," Blanchard did not this time hamper his craft with useless oars and sails. He took with him only a small black dog, some scientific gadgets, and a flag—for it was *de rigueur* for balloon pilots to wave a flag, especially on formal or inaugural flights. This one bore on one side the tricolor of the new French Republic and on the other the Stars and Stripes. As he rose, he detected below him a vast sea of enthusiasm. "Accustomed as I have long been," he wrote, "to the pompous scenes of numerous assemblies, yet I could not help being surprised and astonished when, elevated at a certain height over the city, I turned my eyes towards the immense number of people, which covered the open places, the roofs of the houses, the steeples, the streets and the roads, over which my flight carried me in the free space of the air. What a sight! How delicious for me to enjoy it!" He ascended rapidly and in forty-six minutes crossed the

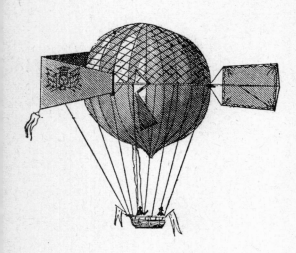

Delaware River and settled down, fifteen miles away, near the village of Woodbury, New Jersey. At least one citizen of this community was unimpressed. "Great ado with looking for and at the Balloon," Samuel Mickle noted in his diary, adding tartly: "This is an instance of the body also as well as the mind being in the air."

Even while Europe was smoking amid the Napoleonic Wars the balloon soared overhead. For Bonaparte's generals formed two companies of *aérostiers*—observers in captive balloons who undertook to direct artillery fire and report on enemy operations; and while these observation posts were of dubious military value, psychologically they made as brave a show as Hannibal's elephants. (Efforts to exploit the balloon for military purposes never did count for much. In 1849 the Austrians were to attempt to bomb Venice with unmanned Montgolfières, without success. Some use was to be made of balloons by the Union Army in the Civil War. Perhaps the most significant operation was to be undertaken by the French during the siege of Paris by the Prussians in 1870–71: sixty-six balloons lifted nine tons of mail and more than a hundred French leaders—including Premier Gambetta—out of the beleaguered city.)

And after the Napoleonic Wars the balloon came back again to its former glory—but with a difference. For it was no longer the scientists and explorers who rode the skies; now it was the showmen. For a time they rode at the caprice of the new emperor. There was André Jacques Garnerin, for example, the first man to make a descent by parachute from a balloon: Napoleon dubbed him *Aérostier des Fêtes Publiques*, in which capacity he presided over the launching of a gaudy aerostat to celebrate the imperial coronation. After Garnerin fell from favor, there was Mme Madeleine-Sophie Blanchard, on whom was conferred the honor of piloting a magnificently decorated balloon to celebrate Napoleon's marriage to Marie Louise of Austria.

Mme Blanchard was a singular woman. The widow of the Blanchard who had first crossed the Channel by air, she appears to have been markedly neurotic. She was an insomniac; she detested noise; she was reluctant to travel about by carriage. To escape from these anxieties she contrived for herself the soothing release of flights in a balloon: she delighted especially in floating through the silent night, far above the world, all by herself. At all events, she was a most popular professional aeronaut, receiving in 1814 from Louis XVIII the title of Official Aeronaut of the Restoration. She was one of the first to touch off fireworks from her balloon, and this was also the cause of her death; for one night in 1819 the hydrogen above her caught fire from one of her displays and she plummeted to a roof in the Rue de Provence. She lies in the Père-Lachaise cemetery under a tombstone on which it is carved that she died "*victime de son art et de son intrépidité.*"

In muted fashion, their thunder stolen by the showmen, a few scientists and a few featherbrains still sought ways to direct the balloon's flight. A Viennese proposed that great eagles be harnessed to the gondola; two Swiss constructed a vast balloon in the shape of a fish, moved by the mad hope that the shape would influence direction; men experimented with clockwork, with steam; they designed airships to fly across the Atlantic and even around the world; but none of these nineteenth-century dreams moved off the drawing board.

In truth, the balloon had been arrogated by show-offs, and even these lively folk were hard put to it to concoct new and striking routines. Fireworks palled. For a time there was a flurry of parachuting animals from balloons, but nobody ever found this very amusing; and one householder in Hampstead, England, got so huffy when a cat was parachuted into his garden as to demand three guineas indemnification for trespass. (He collected, too.) Then for a time there was a fad of equestrian ascensions, an unseemly practice that seems to have been invented by a Frenchman, Testu Brissy, who was also the first aeronaut to attempt a night flight. When horses no longer provoked more than a shrug of the shoulder, someone even soared up astride a stag; and a lady aeronaut was dissuaded from going up as Europa on a Bull only when she was summarily hauled up before a magistrate and severely lectured.

There seemed no end to the brazen indignities to be visited upon the lovely balloon. Naturally Paris was the scene of the first aerostatic duel: a M. de Grandpré and a M. le Pique, having quarreled over the favors of a lady from the Imperial Opera, determined to settle their affair by whanging away at each other with blunderbusses a few thousand feet up. Le Pique fired first and missed, but De Grandpré hit his adversary's balloon, and Le Pique and his foolhardy second were dashed to pieces. Naturally, the United States was the scene of the first aerostatic wedding (in New York, in 1865), complete with parson, bride, groom, best man, and matron of honor. Too often the balloon was piloted by vulgarity, hoax, and sensation.

Somewhere along the line, the wonder and the innocence and the charm and the gaiety that had been hallmarks of early ballooning had been mislaid. However, they were not irretrievably lost. They can always be found again on the face of a child holding that lineal descendant of the original Montgolfière, his first toy balloon.

A FLOAT OF EARLY BALLOONS

EIGHT PAGES OF CONTEMPORARY PRINTS

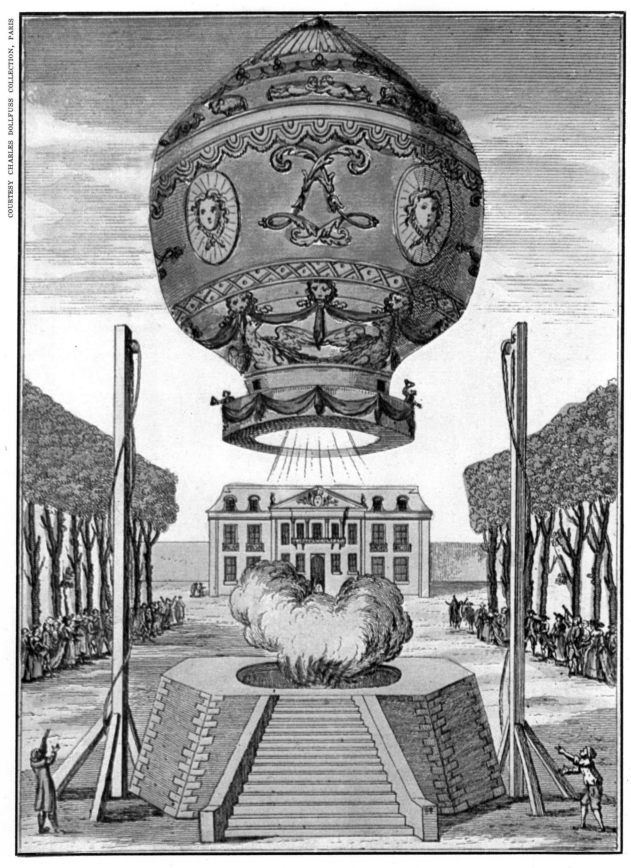

Man's first free ascent from earth, in November, 1783: Pilâtre de Rozier and the Marquis d'Arlandes wave from the gallery of their Montgolfière as they set out from Paris. Their balloon had been inflated with air heated over the fire pit in the foreground, and before it was released a brazier was placed inside the balloon's neck to maintain the heat.

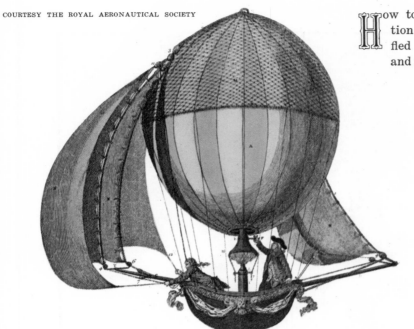

How to establish control over speed and direction of a free balloon was a problem that baffled the aeronauts. This is an early (1785) and fanciful suggestion of how it might be done.

Crossing the Channel in 1785 was a feat compara[ble] to Lindbergh's, later. Blanchard and Jeffries a[re] here leaving Dover Castle on their journey [to] France, where they were enthusiastically cheere[d].

As an official aeronaut, Mme Blanchard, wife of the pilot of the first Channel crossing, floats over the procession bringing Louis XVIII to his throne in Paris in the 1814 Restoration.

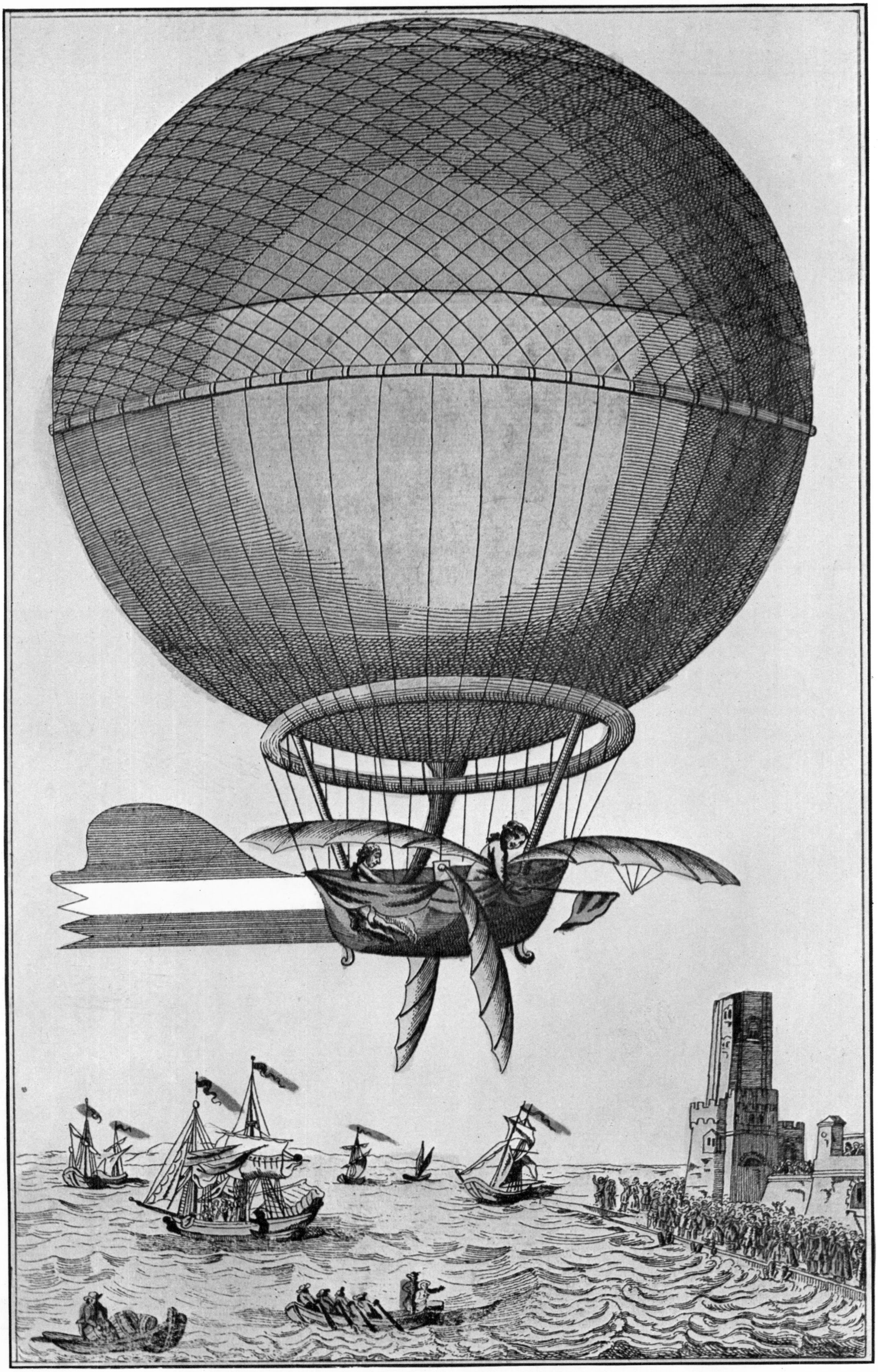

proposal made in Vienna in 1801 was that of harnessing eagles to bring about directional flight.

The first hydrogen balloon (right), which carried Professor Charles and a companion twenty-seven miles from Paris in December, 1783, returns to the city as throngs cheer. With the use of this gas, balloon development began. Below, Blanchard waves the flag to Philadelphians as he starts the first aerial voyage in America (1793).

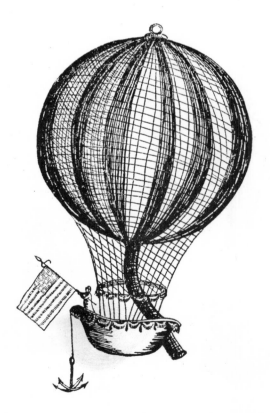

The first equestrian ascent was made in 1798 by the Frenchman Testu Brissy, who trained his horse to stand still on a platform and started a fashion in stunting that lasted many years.

Pilâtre de Rozier, the pioneer aeronaut, experiments with inhaling and exhaling "inflammable air," or hydrogen. When trying a Channel crossing in 1785, he became the first air casualty.

An "Aero-Montgolfière" was built by Francesco Orlandi of Bologna around 1828. The top half was filled with hydrogen, the lower half with hot air. The lower section, with its triangular oars, rudder, and flat top, was to serve as a parachute in an emergency.

French and English caricaturists made sport of balloon mania. One proposed that ladies wear a balloon hat and inflated panniers.

George Cruikshank satirized the balloon craze in this "Scene in the Farce of 'Lofty Projects' as performed with great success for the Benefit & Amusement of John Bull, 1825," in which he also ridiculed the inflated money speculation, or "bubbles."